Writing Magazine and Newspaper Articles

Barbara Braidwood
Richard Cropp
Susan M. Boyce

Self-Counsel Press
(a division of)
International Self-Counsel Press Ltd.
USA   Canada

Self-Counsel Press acknowledges the financial support of the Government of Canada through the Book Publishing Industry Development Program (BPIDP) for our publishing activities.

Printed in Canada.

First edition: January 1999

Canadian Cataloguing in Publication Data
Braidwood, Barbara, 1952–
    Writing magazine and newspaper articles

    (Self-counsel writing series)
    ISBN 1-55180-193-0

    1. Journalism — Authorship.
I. Cropp, Richard, 1952- II. Boyce, Susan M., 1956- I. Title. II. Series.
PN147.B72 1999   808'06607 C98-911079-6

The graphic on page 77 by M. M. Brown (shown in Figure 1) is used by permission.
The excerpt on page 87 by Manuel Erickson is used by permission.
The excerpt on page 91 by Kim Applegate is used by permission.
The sample letter on page 177 by Arthur G. White is used by permission.

Self-Counsel Press
(a division of)
International Self-Counsel Press Ltd.

1704 N. State Street
Bellingham, WA 98225
USA

1481 Charlotte Road
North Vancouver, BC V7J 1H1
Canada

Contents

Samples

Figures

Acknowledgments

Our thanks go to all those writers and editors who took the time to talk to us about their writing experiences: Barbara Beckley, Laura Daily, Lee Foster, Barbara Gibbs Ostmann, Brad Hamilton, Melissa Harmon, Susan Hauser, George Hobica, Mary Lou Janson, Chris Jones, Eve Lazarus, Judi Lees, Neal Matthews, Amy McCloskey, Maureen McFadden, Isabel Nanton, Stan Patty, Nona Piorkowski, Chris Samson, and Lori Todd. Special thanks to Kasey Wilson and Alison Ashton for their efforts and contacts.

Introduction

There is a certain cachet to seeing your words in print. Although we all know words can lie, in our hearts we still believe if something is written down, it is true. We think published writers must know something we do not, because someone has paid them for their words. In fact, publishing just a single article can give the writer a reputation as an expert in the eyes of many people.

Whether you are a hobbyist with a bright idea, a craftsperson with a new technique, have just begun your career, or are a seasoned professional, having your writing published will bring you unexpected rewards. If some aspects of your life are not giving you a sense of fulfillment or you are simply looking for a fresh perspective on life, now is the time to get cracking on an article for publication. The new perspective comes automatically with exciting opportunities — such as research trips and invitations to seminars and press conferences — that arise from publishing articles. After you have a few articles in print, such an opportunity will come to you, probably from a stranger who has read your writing. It has happened to each of us, and it is just as exciting when it happens now as it was the first time it happened.

In this book, we will show you how you can get your articles printed in magazines and newspapers. By taking advantage of our suggestions, ideas, and pointers, you can enjoy the satisfaction of seeing your ideas and words in print. Very few people go through the hard work of writing a good article without the hope that they will influence someone. It is not enough just to have your article appear anywhere in print. The *Siberian Cultural Review* might be a venerable newspaper but how many people does it reach? To be most effective, your article needs to be placed strategically and carefully, and you must shamelessly exploit each success.

Not all published writers are gifts to the literary world, so how did they manage to appear in print? While a writer must be competent, it is just as important to know how to submit articles to the right place at the right time. What most people don't realize is that many good but unpublished writers never take the time to learn how to work the publishing game. As a result, these writers never see their ideas reach anyone else.

Editors at major magazines and newspapers spend a portion of each week looking for articles to fill the pages of their publications. They need a continuous supply of scintillating copy to attract readers and advertisers. If you have a new idea (or a different twist on an old idea) that is well written and timely, editors will pay to use your article — provided you know how to get their attention.

This book shows you how to analyze magazines and newspapers to increase your chances of attracting an editor's attention and being published. It also gives you tips on how to write your article, shows you how and when to submit your article, and points out how to capitalize on your success.

We weren't always in the writing business. Each of us began working in other fields and came to writing by accident or design. We all now have one thing in common, though: publishing articles in magazines and newspapers has provided us with thousands of dollars of extra income, peer recognition, and a lot of fun. As a direct result of our efforts to appear in print, we have been places and done things many people only dream about. If you are looking for exciting experiences and financial rewards for the effort you expend, skip buying lottery tickets and start writing articles. We promise what comes your way will challenge and amaze you.

Part I

The World of Magazines and Newspapers

1

The Rewards of Writing Articles

You've just invested the price of this book in your future as a writer of magazine and newspaper articles. Now you simply have to commit to doing two more things and you will be on your way.

First and easiest is to read this book from cover to cover. Second, don't give up your dream of becoming a published writer. If you persevere, you will succeed.

We have written this book for both novice writers who need a guide through the publishing maze and for nonprofessional writers who may have published a few articles but need a broader view of the publishing world to continue building their careers. By the end of this book, we hope that you will have a good grasp of what you need to do to be published and that you will have acquired a new attitude about your writing projects in general.

If you are not able to get your article published as quickly as you had hoped, consider some of the many benefits of almost any writing exercise. Through your efforts to generate articles, you will be exposed to all kinds of new experiences and will learn new skills such as marketing and copy writing, which will definitely be useful for you down the road. You will also get a glimpse of other interesting professions such as hosting radio or television shows and you will discover the inner workings of different subjects you choose to write about. Along the way, you will meet interesting people and encounter some unusual situations, all of which will be excellent future material and inspiration.

While it is important to know how to write an article and where to send it, the most important thing is to have a broad perspective on what you are doing or trying to do with your writing. Are you writing for recognition at your job, searching for a new career, or keeping busy during your retirement? In the end, this outlook will bring you far more than you had originally envisioned when you sat down to write your first article.

Like many writers, the three of us started out in fields completely unrelated to writing. None of us studied creative writing or English literature, nor did we go to journalism school. However, with perseverance and a little luck, we have all arrived at the point where each of us makes our living from writing. We started by getting one or two articles published in magazines and newspapers, and slowly learned to craft a marketable product.

Some of you will want to write an article just for the sake of expressing your idea. The following are some *other* reasons for writing.

a. Expose yourself to opportunities while earning money

Once you have been published, you have a better chance of being published again, and making money from your writing. Also, by constructing and using a biography that highlights your accomplishments in publishing articles and by using your bio liberally, wonderful opportunities can come your way. (See chapter 22 for more on writing your bio.)

b. Meet new people and share your passion

By writing an article on something you're passionate about, you will meet others who share your passion. If you get a thrill out of showing your latest discovery, you will probably love writing articles about it. If you find your dinner companion's eyes glazing over as you describe your latest discovery about the bone structure of archaeopteryx (a winged dinosaur) or the brilliance of

Jackson's lightning flanking movement at Chancellorsville, you probably need to save that conversation to have with the new people you meet.

Beginning with the librarian who helps find obscure articles for you when you are doing advance research for an interview you dream of having with a famous person, new people will enter your life when you write.

c. Encounter new challenges

Looking for something new to do? Want to spice up your work-a-day world? Write an article. Not only is the writing a challenge — it can be both difficult *and* satisfying — but you learn a new set of skills.

The best part is you can start with no money and just a little time. You don't need courses, permission to start, a job interview, acceptance by an institution of higher learning, or even a degree. Just grab a piece of paper and a pen and let loose your desire to take on something new. Along the way, you will learn about writing, interviewing, researching, computer technology, and a host of other new stuff.

d. Become an expert

When you have spent years delving into a particular subject you naturally learn far more about it than people not in that field. Gradually you become an expert. Of course, there are millions of experts. Anyone who has worked twenty years in accounts payable is an expert on the company's accounting system. The difference between your run-of-the-mill expert who has toiled quietly for years accumulating knowledge and an acknowledged expert is simply public recognition of the set of skills the person has acquired. Writing articles can help gain that public recognition for you. This book shows you how.

e. Earn recognition and credibility

There is a hierarchy in the publishing world among newspapers and magazines. Having your article appear in the *Wall Street Journal* will certainly get you a favorable reaction from your colleagues. Prestige may be important to achieving your goals; we

A published article can be a stamp of approval. Imagine the future résumé of the student whose class science project is featured in the Journal of the American Medical Association, *the foremost medical journal in the United States.*

will show you how to assess the relative merits of different publications.

Of course, if you have dozens of published articles to your credit, even in smaller publications, that counts too. Even one published article, clipped and given to, for example, your boss can put you in a new light in his or her eyes.

It's no wonder the tabloids featured near the grocery store checkouts have such huge circulations. Many years of schooling have taught us the written word is always true. This training is so powerful that the simple fact of something being written down often gives it a credibility that's impossible to shake.

This belief can lead to some peculiar attitudes. Your poker chums might not believe what you say on a subject, but once your words are in print, chances are excellent they will believe what you have written. You might not be able to talk your coworkers into implementing your new ideas, but just watch the change in attitude when you express those same ideas in print.

f. Add new dimensions to your life

As a published writer, new horizons open up for you. With publication comes a newfound sense that you really can reach farther than before and that just about anything is possible. This may sound quite unreal, but it can have a profound influence on the direction of your life. For example, you may never have imagined it was possible to meet a legend in your field, but as a writer, you may have access to that person for an interview. You may have a hard time justifying the expense of a trip to Europe for a conference on your favorite subject just because you are interested in it, but the fact that you can write an article on the conference and may make money by selling the article might be enough incentive for you to go ahead and make the trip.

These examples show a different way of looking at the world and your place in it. As a published writer, you can shift your mindset and spend time seriously thinking about how to accomplish what were merely daydreams before. Once you've had a little success turning your daydreams into reality, your horizons begin to expand dramatically. And once you really believe it is possible for you to interview the president or prime minister or spend time with the real Dr. Baker (of *Jurassic Park* fame), your creative juices will begin to boil and new ideas will surface. You'll find yourself thinking about other articles and ways of presenting your ideas and how you can accomplish your goals.

This is a gradual process that eventually becomes part of your life. This new way of thinking about the world is perhaps the best part of publishing your writing.

g. Experience a thrill

There is no question — you will experience a real thrill when your first article is published. Each subsequent time you're published, you'll feel that same thrill. You'll also experience a thrill the first time someone invites you on an all-expenses-paid trip to speak at a conference or to experience a particular product. Depending on what you are writing about, you may be deluged with free food, clothes, stereos, or trips. Write enough and these offers can become a nuisance rather than a thrill. Writers who write travel articles complain about having to take yet another cruise while food writers complain about getting fat. If you follow our suggestions closely, you can have these problems too.

2

Magazines or Newspapers — Which One Is for You?

This chapter is designed to give you some idea of the differences between magazines and newspapers. There will, inevitably, be exceptions to these generalizations. Still, there is enough truth and substance to these hints that you should bear them in mind when you are looking for a publisher.

The production of newspapers is generally much faster paced than magazines. Since many newspapers are published daily, newspaper employees are usually scrambling. Magazines are created in a more genteel and deliberate fashion. Keep this difference foremost in your mind as you plan your writing strategy. Most writers tend to favor writing for either one or the other.

a. Article length

Weekday newspapers are aimed primarily at readers with very little time and the articles tend to be short and snappy. Articles of just 50 to 75 words are not uncommon. Weekend newspapers tend to be more like their magazine cousins in that there is space devoted to longer, more analytical or literary pieces, which usually means an increase in the word count of the articles.

Most magazine articles tend to be 500 to 750 words long, although they can be longer depending on the magazine and the writer. For example, investigative journalism articles or pieces written by well-known people often have more space dedicated to them. Many magazines have departments or columns where each item is only 50 to 75 words but, on the whole, magazine articles are longer than newspaper articles.

Pay attention to the guidelines provided to you by the newspaper or magazine. (For more detailed information on guidelines and how to obtain them, see chapter 19.) You might also count the number of words in several of the publication's articles to get a sense of what is required. The fastest way to have your article rejected is to send in an article of totally inappropriate word count. No editor has the time to carefully pare your article to the desired length. Newspaper editors particularly may have two or three column inches in their layout that they need to fill and they want exactly enough words to fill the space.

The writing style for newspaper articles is usually more abbreviated than that of their magazine counterparts. Short paragraphs and short sentences are the standard.

b. Writing style

There's clearly a difference in style between magazines and newspapers, but there is also a difference in style between various magazines and between various newspapers. For example, the style of the *Wall Street Journal* is very different from that of the *National Enquirer*. In general, though, newspapers tend to want short, concise sentences organized in bite-size paragraphs. You'll probably want to use simple, declarative sentences and fairly uncomplicated phrases and words in your newspaper articles. The exceptions to this are the opinion and editorial pages which often feature more detailed and densely constructed sentences and articles.

Magazine article writing tends to be more elaborate and detailed so as a rule, you're more likely to find long, complex words in a magazine than in a newspaper.

Of course, general descriptions of newspaper and magazine style are just that — generalizations to which there are numerous exceptions. Some magazines exhibit a short, point-form style while some newspapers go to great lengths to express the writer's point of view. The best advice we can give you as to read your target publication to ascertain the flavor of the publication.

c. Pace of writing

If you are a slow, deliberate writer, write for magazines. If you become a regular contributor, most magazine editors will give you lots of advance notice for a piece they would like you to do.

With newspaper writing, you'll rarely be so fortunate. It is not uncommon for a newspaper editor to call you and ask for 250 words to fill a blank spot in the layout. The newspaper's editor will make it very clear that he or she is staring at the blank spot waiting for your words, so the sooner you get them in, the sooner the editor can go home to dinner.

d. Dealing with personnel

The difference in pace at magazines and newspapers makes for some distinctions in how editors in the two fields are likely to deal with you. At the outset of your relationship with a publication, ask your editor when his or her deadline days are and write them down. Unless it is emergency related to your article, do not call your editor on these days.

Next, although it may seem that all editors are victims of bipolar personality disorder — happy to talk to you one day, grumpy and curt the next — don't take it personally. The pressure on editors to perform accurately and quickly is intense and can arise unexpectedly. You can win friends by keeping an upbeat tone and not holding grudges.

All writers are somewhat insecure about their product and need just a little extra attention or reassurance from time to time. Ask a writing friend, not your editor, for this type of support. Your editor's job is to fill the publication as efficiently as possible, not critique your writing in great detail *and* guide your career. The fact that the magazine or newspaper has published your work and sent you a check is the only approval you can expect. Anything else amounts to hand-holding and is not part of the contract.

Finally, you'll have to judge whether your editor wants more contact with you, such as an occasional lunch, or to see your face in the office from time to time. However, don't be surprised if years go by between face-to-face meetings. Barbara and Rick were once hired by an editor who they wrote for regularly but saw only every couple of years. You will meet writers who have never met their editors who work on the other side of the country.

e. Editing changes

Many writers have a fear of seeing their name above an article that has been edited to the point that the meaning of their words has been changed entirely. If this is a particular concern of yours, stick with magazines. Newspapers are produced so quickly, it is unlikely you will see the edited version of your article before it goes to press. There just isn't time to get a piece through the editing process, contact you, wait for your response, argue about the changes, incorporate your changes, and get it into print in a few days or hours.

f. Using e-mail

Newspaper editors usually like to receive queries by e-mail because e-mail suits the fast-paced atmosphere of most newspaper offices. Many newspaper editors say they answer their e-mail before they answer faxes or regular mail because it's easy to dash off a two-line response and be done with the chore. Magazine editors tend to be split on the issue of using e-mail for queries. The less frantic pace of magazine publishing is more conducive to opening regular mail.

g. Invoicing and payment

With rare exceptions, both magazines and newspapers pay only on publication. Both usually also require an invoice to be sent to the editor (or the accounting department) before payment is made. Always ask whom to send your invoice to when you submit your manuscript.

Because of the basic difference in timelines, you will find the biggest difference between newspapers and magazines is that newspapers may publish your article within a few days of submission whereas with magazines you may wait several months to be published.

3

Decisions, Decisions. What to Write.

Be prepared for your life as an article writer to be somewhat erratic, often frenzied, and anything but dull. Writing articles is an endlessly varied profession, and while many writers specialize, few specialize in one subject to the point of excluding all others. It's part of the enjoyment to be writing about killer whales one day and killer soccer games the next.

There is probably a category for any topic you can think of. Here are some common ones to get you thinking about which type of article you may want to write. There will always be crossovers between categories.

a. How-to articles

How to build a boat, cook a tastier pancake, have better sex, learn a foreign language — the list is endless. How-to articles are perennial favorites among readers, editors, and writers, and no matter how many times someone has written about a given subject, there will always be an editor who wants to run a piece on it.

For an aspiring writer, how-to articles can be an easy way to start building that all-important portfolio of published credits.

Here are some points to keep in mind as you help teach people how to do the things they want to do.

(a) *Present the information in chronological order.* You can still go for a catchy lead, but you won't have much choice in ordering your material once you start actually explaining how it's done.

(b) *Never assume your readers are familiar with the basics.* If they were, they probably wouldn't be reading your article in the first place. Even the most highly educated and worldly wise person will be a novice at something.

A few years ago, Susan was finishing a contract job in a client's office. She asked one of the women in the office if she wouldn't mind running downstairs and putting another dollar in Susan's parking meter as the time was about to run out. Fifteen minutes later, the woman wasn't yet back. Finally, after almost twenty-five minutes, she returned. Because of a physical disability, the woman didn't drive, and so she had no idea what to do when the parking meter's handle stuck slightly. This example illustrates how easy it is to take for granted things you are familiar with.

(c) *Provide diagrams or other necessary illustrations.* Even if you can't draw, a few rough sketches will be greatly appreciated by most editors. If you have photos, so much the better.

(d) *Keep it simple.* How-to articles are not the place for long, languorous prose or epic historical details. Use basic language with appropriate, accurate terminology (a quarter teaspoon of salt rather than the classic pinch).

b. Reviews

Writing reviews is fun and frequently offers great perks in the form of free stuff — books, theater tickets, sporting equipment, and meals. To write about something, you usually have to have some experience with it, and the producer of the product is usually willing to give away the product in exchange for a review.

Reviews can be not only lucrative, they can also be a relatively easy way to break into print, especially if you approach smaller local newspapers. If you love reading, write three or four sample

No matter what area you decide to write in, always double check your facts and figures. Although some large publications do have fact-checking departments, many don't, and small publications rarely do. It is your responsibility as a writer to be accurate.

book reviews and submit them to the appropriate editor along with a proposal to write one or two more reviews for future issues.

Let your imagination go wild as you think of things to review. Here are a few ideas for review topics to help you get started:

- coffee shop artwork
- grocery stores
- hotels
- local gardens
- local hiking trails
- martial arts tournaments
- movies or videos
- nightclubs
- parks
- pets
- pubs
- restaurants
- school sports events
- TV shows/movies

As you get set to write your review, keep these points in mind.

(a) *Be honest in your review.* Don't be afraid to be up-front about the good, the bad, and yes, even the ugly. Don't feel you must say the book was wonderful just because everyone else is saying so. But remember, you must adequately support why you rate a product or event the way you do. You must say, "It was wonderful/terrible/delicious/sour/overpriced *because...*"

(b) *Don't use filler descriptions.* "The painting is pretty" doesn't really tell the reader anything because everyone's idea of pretty is different. "The painting has a bold mix of primary colors and subtle shading" provides readers with more concrete grounds for deciding if they want to attend an art exhibit or not.

(c) *Provide detailed information.* Be sure to include any pertinent details such as price, location, size, where the product is available, and for how long. These details will, naturally, depend on what you are reviewing.

(d) *Accentuate something positive.* No matter how disappointing you feel the event or item was, it is always a good idea to try to find one good thing about whatever it is you're reviewing. Perhaps the view from the restaurant was lovely or the computer program loaded easily (although you weren't able to run the program because there was no manual) or the book cover was the perfect complement to the storyline. Finding that one positive thing minimizes the chance you'll be perceived as a cynical, cranky writer with an axe to grind.

(e) *Be reasonable.* When you do find yourself having to write a negative review, be sure it's really the product that's bad. Some things are beyond anyone's ability to control, so don't make the whole experience poor quality. If the lead actor was suddenly stricken with appendicitis, the understudy had strep throat, and the only other available person had to read the lines from a script, it's unfair to say the play was poorly produced. The show that night was, understandably, having some troubles, but if the production might otherwise have been excellent, you owe it to your readers to tell them so. (Susan actually attended a play where this happened. Even worse, in the middle of the first act, the brake on a wheelchair being used as a prop failed, leaving another actor with a *real* broken leg, not simply the one the script called for!)

c. Interviews and profiles

Whether the story involves kings and queens or the couple next door, people love reading about people. If you're in any doubt, just take a look at the magazine racks by the checkout counter next time you go grocery shopping. Splashed over the covers of *People* and *Time* and dozens of other magazines are pictures of — you guessed it — people.

The best news is your profile doesn't have to be a one-on-one with an international superstar; there are hundreds of people right in your own neighborhood who you could interview. Even better, most people are quite happy to talk about themselves, so interviewing is often surprisingly easy. Chapter 4 discusses interviewing in more depth.

d. Self-improvement and self-help articles

In today's increasingly competitive world, we are bombarded with admonitions that we should become better — better citizens; better spouses; better at managing our health, our money, our job; and better at surviving illness, abuse, and stress. For writers, this has translated into a powerful demand for articles describing how and why average people need to improve themselves emotionally, physically, financially, and spiritually.

Your career as a self-improvement writer will be helped if you have a series of letters after your name. An M.D., B.Sc., P.Eng., or other recognized accreditation not only offers you the potential to bring in a tidy sum but also helps increase your visibility as an authority on your subject. But don't fret if you're just plain Mary Gray or Martin Green. Many self-improvement and self-help articles are written by laypeople with practical, hands-on experience.

Writing self-help articles actually has some surprising similarities to writing advertising copy. Your job is to sell readers on the benefits of changing some aspect of their lives. Take a look at some articles on subjects as diverse as anger management, drumming, aromatherapy for pain control, and assertiveness in the workplace — they are all selling the benefits of an idea. Keep this in mind as you write.

As with a sales pitch, you should leave no doubt in readers' minds about why they need the information in your article. Perhaps it will help them become more glamorous, live longer, or provide a better life for their children. Whatever it is you're selling in your self-improvement writing, make sure you sell the sizzle. Remember, it's trendy today to be fit in mind, body, and spirit, and that trend can have a positive influence on your bank account's fitness level as well.

Cultivate a few friendships with recognized experts in various fields. They will be able to provide information and add credibility to your articles, and most will be happy to give you referrals to other experts in their field.

The self-improvement and self-help market is not just about exercise and diet. It includes such diverse subjects as alternative healing, meditation and meditative techniques (e.g., yoga and Tai Chi), dealing with addictions, overcoming physical or emotional abuse, communication skills, and relationships.

e. Travel articles

Paris. Rome. The Great Barrier Reef.

Travel's appeal never diminishes and the wonders of foreign lands remain eternal favorites with readers and writers alike. In fact, travel writing is so popular, we've written a book called *Writing Travel Books and Articles* published by Self-Counsel Press on that subject. Here are some pointers to get you going.

(a) *Be descriptive.* The best travel articles help readers experience the destination as they read, so be as lavish in your descriptions as suits your personal style. "We went into a quaint restaurant and ate delicious lobster," doesn't create an ambience. Thousands of towns have quaint restaurants and delicious lobster. Besides, one person may believe quaint means Victorian chintz and lace, while another may visualize the funky (did someone say tacky?) plastic and arborite of the 1950's retro look.

Try instead:

At a wobbly table covered with blue gingham and crowned with a basket of scarlet carnations, we savored fresh-caught lobster smothered in herb butter while the sun dipped slowly beneath the Mediterranean waters.

Whether or not you like lobster, this description conjures up an appealing atmosphere.

(b) *Get personal.* Avoid telling your readers what "one" is able to do. "One may enjoy lobster on the beach at sunset," is stilted and distancing. Tell people what *you* experienced.

(c) *Be sure your information is current.* One editor we spoke to said she'd received a submission about how to spend two weeks in Rome for only $2,000 including airfare from North America. The problem was, the prices quoted were more than five years out of date. Needless to say, she didn't buy the article and probably tagged the writer as one to avoid in the future.

(d) *Pace yourself.* Avoid the temptation of trying to describe your entire eight-week trek through Patagonia in a 1,200-word article. It can't be done. Instead, pick the single most interesting adventure you had during the journey and use your allotted word count to tell your readers about just that one event. Not only will this produce a much more entertaining and marketable article, but it will leave you with material for dozens more articles.

(e) *Don't forget about home.* Remember your hometown is an exciting foreign land to someone from the other side of the world, possibly even from the other side of the country. Many writers make a good living by writing about attractions within miles of where they live and then selling those stories to magazines and newspapers around the world.

f. Personal essays

Once the darling of many newspapers, personal essays fell from favor somewhere in the mid-1900s. Happily, that trend appears to be reversing and personal essays are once again in vogue.

As the name implies, personal essays are reflections about the self — yourself, your experiences, your life. Often concerning intense emotional experiences, they may refer back to an event that occurred in childhood or a recent triumph. This is where you bare your soul for all to see, so if you're the shy, reserved type, personal essays may not be for you.

Personal essays often begin as journal or diary entries or even letters to a close friend or relative. It is this personal, intimate tone you will want to aim for. In fact, many writers who pursue this type of article write their first draft as a stream of consciousness piece. Also known as free writing, stream of consciousness simply means picking a topic and writing about it for a predetermined length of time.

Let's say you are interested in writing a personal essay about your grade six friendship with a mentally challenged classmate. Hold a picture of that person in your mind for a minute or two, then pick up your pen and begin to write whatever comes to mind. It doesn't matter what it is or how disjointed your thoughts may seem, just keep writing for at least ten minutes or until you feel you are done. Don't stop, don't edit, don't be critical, just keep writing. You may end up with something like this:

> Joey's dark eyes, hair always in his eyes. What a warm smile he always had. That green and blue striped sweater — oh and the funny lunch bucket. I wonder why he never wore purple — maybe his mother didn't like it or was it because of the bike? He was always so proud of the bike. They never did like him but he had such a gentle nature.

Before writing about your hometown, take a few days to play tourist. Go on a guided tour, visit museums and tacky tourist traps, sit in a sidewalk café watching what the other tourists do, and then go off and try the same things. You'll be amazed at how many ideas you'll come up with by exploring right in your own neighborhood.

Laughter. Always laughing and brought the best floats for the parade. Wonder if he made it to Spain?

This original and very raw format will most likely present no useful information to someone other than the writer. For example, what bike? Why did Joey want to go to Spain? And what about the funny lunch bucket? But these questions, once expanded, could form the basis of a delightful personal essay about friendship.

g. Inspirational or spiritual writing

Don't be afraid to use emotionally charged situations or language when you are writing either personal essays or inspirational articles.

Inspirational writing is a close relative of the personal essay. Most frequently written in the first person, these articles are designed to show readers a triumphant resolution to a difficult problem. However, it's important to differentiate between triumphant and victorious. An inspirational article about a cancer patient may still end with that person's death. The triumph comes in the way the person deals with death — giving hope and courage to others who read the article.

Like the personal essay, writing for this market tends to use highly descriptive language to evoke emotion. There is also emphasis on metaphysical matters. Don't shy away from using the religious or supernatural language that is typically avoided in other genres, as long as you don't use it just for the sake of appearing spiritually oriented.

Although inspirational writing frequently includes specific religious references, a direct religious affiliation is not a necessary component, nor do you need to be of a particular faith to write for a magazine of that faith. Susan has written articles for three different religious publications and follows none of their belief systems.

h. Technical writing

Technical writing is often confused with writing scientific research papers. In reality, technical writing is far more closely related to how-to writing. Technical writers produce user manuals, guides, training handbooks, and other organizational tools for communicating technical information to end users. If you're not enthralled with working with complex, multilevel structural outlines, this is an area to avoid, but if you love seeing sections and subsections and subsubsections, this may be an area that's tailor-made for you.

If you're considering pursuing technical writing, you'll need the following qualities over and above writing skill. You must:

- Be a team player — most technical writing is done as part of a team
- Have an exceptional ability to communicate clearly, assertively, and diplomatically
- Be able to take criticism well
- Be meticulous about meeting deadlines
- Remember accuracy and attention to detail come first — always. Imagine the devastating consequences if a manual on storing flammable materials published instructions to store them at 40°C instead of minus 40°C.
- Have a general knowledge of what type of illustrations (graphs, charts, schematics, or line art) will work best with a given project
- Have a general knowledge of the principles of page layout

Your writing style should be crisp and clean. In technical writing, even more than in other types of writing, you must keep your finger firmly on the delete key if you find yourself including wordy descriptions and explanations. Instructions like "Protective eye covering approved by the safety commission should be worn at all times by the user" are cumbersome. "Wear safety-approved goggles" gets to the point immediately.

It is also crucial to be aware of the level of knowledge of your audience. As one technical writer pointed out, not so long ago people actually needed written instructions posted outside an elevator in order to operate it. Obviously, such a sign would be ridiculous in today's society. However, technical writers must not forget our earlier warning about not assuming readers' knowledge.

While technical writing is often perceived as dull and dry, for anyone with an insatiable curiosity about how and why things work the way they do, the constant learning and opportunity to be involved with new information and innovations can bring

Decisions, decisions. What to write.

Some other topics you might want to write about:

- *children and parenting*
- *entertainment*
- *sports*
- *cars, boats, and RVs*
- *gardening*
- *pets*
- *interior decorating*
- *architecture*
- *new-age issues*
- *religion*
- *alternative medicines*
- *gay/lesbian issues*
- *retirement*
- *seniors*
- *medical issues*
- *technical issues*

enormous satisfaction, as well as a healthy paycheck. While many technical writers are employed full time by companies who need a steady stream of technical documentation, be sure to check out the ever-expanding trade publication market if you would like to try to begin as a freelancer in this field.

Our list of different types of magazine and newspaper articles is far from complete and several of the categories overlap. Remember, as a freelance writer, anything that captures your interest has the potential to generate income in the form of an article (or two or three)!

The following chapters focus on some of the specialized fields of magazine and newspaper writing and also provide expert advice from editors and writers in the industry.

4

Interviewing — How to Get Your Story

The thought of interviewing someone for a magazine or newspaper article can fill some writers with dread. The good news is that the more people you interview, the more comfortable you will become doing it.

When you approach a potential interviewee, whether in person or by telephone, explain exactly why you would like to speak with him or her, what topic you want to address, and ask when would be a convenient time. The person you are approaching may be extremely busy when you call or may prefer to have a few hours to think about what he or she will be discussing with you. Always be prepared to set up your interview for another time — even a telephone interview.

There are two schools of thought about the best way to prepare for an interview. One says you should do thorough research and learn everything you possibly can about the subject beforehand; the other says you should find out just the basics so that you will remain open to opportunities to take the interview in various directions, filling in gaps with research later. The reality for most writers is somewhere in the middle of the two extremes, but we've found we lean more toward the second than the first. This is especially true if we are covering a difficult or sensitive issue or one surrounded by controversy. We find this way we go into the interview with fewer preconceived ideas of what we'll find.

For example, when Susan was interviewing a woman whose daughter had been imprisoned in South America on kidnapping charges, controversy had raged around the case for almost seven years. The woman was understandably leery of speaking with the press since many of the articles published had condemned both her and her daughter as liars or worse. Susan's editor had specifically requested an article that showed the personal side of this woman's story without delving too deeply into the politics or ethics involved. Susan decided to do the most basic research before the interview: where, when, and what. Because she made a point of ignoring the plethora of opinion pieces already publish-ed, she was able to remain unbiased during the interview itself.

As you become more comfortable with interviewing, you'll discover your own balance and develop an intuition about how much research to bring to an interview. Here are some other points to keep in mind:

If the idea of interviewing a stranger or a celebrity leaves you weak-kneed with fright, take a few minutes every day to talk to yourself in front of a mirror. Does the person looking out at you appear interested? Does he or she seem friendly and approachable? If not, practice until you are pleased with the results.

(a) *Always be courteous.* Even if your interviewee will benefit from the publicity your article will create for him or her, that person is still doing you a favor by agreeing to meet with you and give you his or her time.

(b) *Listen more than you speak.* If you do all the talking, you'll have nothing to write about and may alienate the person you were speaking with.

(c) *Look interested.* Maintain good eye contact, smile, nod in agreement, make clucking sounds if it's appropriate, and show the interviewee you are paying attention and are interested in what he or she is telling you to the exclusion of anything else that's going on around you.

(d) *Don't be afraid of silence.* Let the silence hang — especially when you're getting into the heart of the interview. People get nervous when they are about to reveal something im-portant and will often pause before proceeding. Fortunately, most people get even more nervous when there is a long pause in a conversation, so, as an interviewer, avoid being the person to break that silence. When you sense your subject is about to let you in on the big scoop, this is the time to keep your ears open and your mouth firmly shut.

(e) *Ask open-ended questions.* "How did you feel when you realized you had just won $1 million?" will yield far more material than "Were you excited when you won $1 million?"

(f) *Break the ice.* Begin with a few minutes of general conversation before beginning the business part of an interview. Commenting on the family dog or admiring the awards in the interviewee's display cabinet helps put your interviewee at ease and allows him or her to relate to you as a person rather than as "the Press." One word of warning: Some people love to chat for hours. Be prepared to gently but firmly begin the formal interview within a few minutes of meeting.

(g) *Remain detached.* Don't allow yourself to be drawn into the controversy or emotions surrounding the topic. Your job is to find out the interviewee's opinions, thoughts, and feelings, not to express yours or get into an argument. It's sometimes difficult to remain outside the subject, especially when it's one you feel passionate about, but if you allow yourself to get emotional, your article will almost certainly suffer for it.

(h) *Avoid comments made "off the record."* However, once you've agreed to keep comments off the record, keep your promise.

(i) *Watch for interesting side issues.* Sometimes an interviewee will mention a tidbit of information in passing that can add unexpected depth to your article or even create a whole other article. In Susan's interview that we mentioned earlier, the mother was discussing what she went through when she visited her daughter. Tucked in with comments about having to open parcels and show official passes, she added, "and, of course, the strip search isn't very nice either." The comment was so matter-of-fact, Susan almost missed it. Susan immediately asked for clarification and, in the end, felt it had such emotional impact she wrote it into the lead to her story.

(j) *Don't shy away from interviewing celebrities.* While it's true some celebrities are difficult to deal with, are arrogant, and may be downright rude to the press, it's often because the press has been unnecessarily intrusive or inaccurate in its reports. Most celebrities are courteous, well mannered, and well spoken. This is not, however, to say they will volunteer

Most publications do not want a writer to use a source that cannot be identified. As a writer, you need to be able to justify who your source is. As a beginning writer, if your source insists on remaining confidential, find another one. However, as your reputation as a scrupulous, efficient writer grows, it will be easier to write without having to reveal your sources.

every piece of information you might like to have in your article. Be prepared for the times when an interviewee simply will not talk about a certain subject and respect his or her privacy.

(k) *Learn how to tape an interview.* A microcassette tape recorder is considered essential equipment by many seasoned interviewers. Especially if you don't write quickly or don't know shorthand, taping an interview helps you to conduct the interview without having to write, listen, and worry about keeping the interview on track all at the same time.

The downside occurs when you have to transcribe the notes, which effectively doubles the amount of time spent on each interview, or when you're searching for that quote you just know will make a wonderful introduction and have to fast-forward through several tapes to find it. Tape recorders also make some interviewees feel self-conscious, which may mean they speak less freely during the interview.

We generally rely on a tape recorder as well as note taking. That way, if we want to double check exactly what our subject said, the interview is there to be replayed. But we can use our notes to avoid the lengthy process of going through every word on the tape.

If you plan to use a tape recorder, remember the following:

- Always carry spare batteries and more blank tapes than you think you'll possibly need. It's a well-known fact machines of all sorts break down at the most inopportune moments.

- Be discrete. Avoid fussing with the recorder unnecessarily and try not to have it placed too conspicuously between you and your interviewee.

- Test your equipment before you arrive. The time to find out you have a problem is before the interview, not halfway through it. You'd be amazed how often people forget this simple precaution and lose the best part of an interview because of it.

(l) *Use quotes appropriately.* Quotes can add another dimension to an article, but only if they are from someone worth quoting. A dog groomer would be a logical person to interview

If you have trouble ignoring distractions while taking notes during an interview, practice in front of the evening news or during a movie.

If you're taking notes during an interview, keep writing. When you go for long periods without writing anything at all, it's a subtle, psychological signal to your interviewee that what he or she is saying isn't worth noting. Even if you're jotting down your grocery list, keep your pen in motion.

for an article on pet care; a computer expert who's never owned a pet other than a mouse wouldn't be.

If you're quoting word for word, always use quotation marks and indicate who the quote is attributed to, as in the following example:

"The sky is falling," says Henny Penny, astrologist with the local branch of the Mother Goose Institute.

Otherwise, paraphrase the sentence:

Henny Penny, astrologist with the Mother Goose Institute, indicated Friday that she believes the sky may fall later this year.

One final note about writing interview articles. Many editors do not like interviewees to see the finished article before it goes to print. Even though an interviewee may have agreed to the interview knowing he or she will be on record, the temptation to suggest improvements and changes to your article is just too strong for some. On rare occasions, interviewees will even become belligerent about making changes.

It is, however, perfectly acceptable and, in fact, advisable to check on details and accuracy with your interviewee before you send in the final copy. A short, professional call can save you endless headaches and troubles later!

5

Adventure Writing

Travel is one of the fastest-growing industries in the United States and Canada, and adventure travel, in particular, is skyrocketing in popularity. As an example, the number of people enjoying kayaking and other paddle sports (virtually unknown except amongst aficionados ten years ago) has more than doubled in the last decade. Mountain climbing, the sport of lunatics a decade ago, is featured in dozens of bestselling books, and Mount Everest expeditions are regularly featured in the media. It is no longer unusual for newspapers to buy feature stories about crazy subjects like BASE jumping (parachuting from buildings, aerials, spans, and escarpments), and entire magazines are now devoted to adventure subjects. This has created new markets and travel opportunities for novice and experienced writers.

In addition, this is one area where extensive experience taking photographs is essential. Not only can you earn extra cash for your picture (sometimes more than for the article itself), but the majority of adventure articles must be accompanied by photos to stand a chance of being published. Your pictures don't have to be of professional quality but they do need to augment the story. See chapter 13 for photography tips.

a. Hard versus soft adventure

Adventure writing breaks down into hard and soft adventure. Soft adventures, such as commercial river rafting or sea kayaking, pose

It has become popular (and smart) to challenge the wilderness with a full entourage of bearers and cooks whose duty it is to rescue you and your belongings should you wander off and who will do all the grunt work while you happily snap photos.

a minimal threat to your health: an element of danger exists but most of the unknowns have been dealt with by an expert who is there to guide you. Of course, the beauty of soft adventure is that there is a possibility for it to unexpectedly become hard adventure.

As the name suggests, hard adventure has more to do with hard things like rocks, splints, casts, and coffins, though some adventure writers claim it actually has to do with another aspect of the research. As one panting writer put it after a close call, "It was more exciting than sex, even with my wife." Hard adventure writing can range from a tour of a war-torn country to an article on a Mount Everest expedition.

Many mainstream publications now include articles with a bit of sizzle, excitement, blood, and gore to capitalize on the thrill of soft adventure. They know that their readers, especially the baby boomers, are interested in adventure and excitement and many of those readers see themselves taking smaller risks than those involved in trekking to Nepal and undergoing the tortured ascent of a dangerous peak. What this means for you as a writer is you have a much wider market than you did a few years ago and that market appears to be expanding further.

Adventure writing is basically travel writing with an emphasis on action. In the past, just telling a story about adventure travel was all that was needed for your article to be snapped up by an editor. However, as the genre has matured, writers are now having to come up with something new and different. Many writers have turned to writing articles of practical suggestions on what and how to pack for your sea kayaking trip or tips on how to climb a particularly difficult rock face. Editors these days have seen so many descriptive stories of adventure trips that unless you have a spectacularly riveting story, such as Jon Krakauer's *Into Thin Air*, which chronicles the dreadful days in 1996 when several climbers died while climbing Mount Everest, you don't stand much of a chance of getting published with traditional storytelling. Having said all that, a well-written story on just about any subject will always stand out.

Writing magazine and newspaper articles

b. Sports writing

Adventure writing can also include articles on sports such as skateboarding, mountain biking, hiking, snowboarding, BMX bicycling, wind surfing, running, and Iron Man competitions. Each one of the sports has equipment to be tested and reviewed, techniques to be explained, and locations to be surveyed.

c. Is adventure writing right for you?

Here are some important points to consider before embarking on a career as an adventure writer.

(a) *Are you self-reliant and resourceful?* Adventure writing, more than any other type of writing, can put you, the writer, in situations where your comfort and well-being, sometimes your life, depends on how fast you can adapt to an unknown situation.

(b) *Do you need a bath every day?* There is a correlation between the harshness of an adventure and dirt buildup. Mountain climbers frequently sit in cold, wet tents for days on end waiting for the weather to break. Enjoying moldy munchies is part of the fun. At the very least, you will have to tolerate camping, bugs, bad weather, and no television.

(c) *Do you like physical activity?* No adventure story was ever written in the pub. Most adventures happen out there somewhere and require a bit of energy expenditure.

(d) *Do you like the great outdoors?* With the exception of spelunking, most of what you write about will be out in the elements.

(e) *Can your body take the punishment?* If your friends frequently refer to you as a klutz or you are generally not healthy, find a different field to write about. Even with soft adventure stories, the research can be arduous. As you get older and your bones beg for a soft bed, you may be restricted in the kinds of stories you can pursue even if you are able to lighten the hardship you tackle. As a rule, adventure writing is a young person's game.

(f) *Do you have good judgment about the risks you take on?* Some people have a hard time understanding their limits and take on more than they should. If you put yourself in this type of situation and are able to pull it off, great. You will have challenged yourself and gained some confidence and skills. However, placing yourself in a tenuous situation through poor judgment can lead to a thoroughly rotten experience and could even result in risk or injury to yourself and those in your party.

d. Sponsoring your adventure

Sponsorship is important to all types of magazine and newspaper article writers. It is particularly critical to adventure writers and food writers. While there are always some adventure stories lurking in your backyard, once you have exhausted those ideas that are close by and don't require expensive equipment, you'll have to look farther afield for the extra money for travel costs, equipment, and other research expenses. Becoming a savvy procurer of sponsorship will make all the difference in the quality and publishability of your stories.

1. Finding a sponsor

Contrary to the advice we give in the rest of this book to think small and start small, it pays to think a little bigger when contemplating how to gain a sponsor's interest. Most companies have a fixed budget for sponsorship projects for a given year and measure the results of the money that was spent by how many people were reached with the message about their product. This means if your articles are going to appear only in small publications with small circulations, there may not be enough anticipated payback to your potential sponsor for him or her to release funds to you. You may have to go after larger publications or a combination of many smaller publications.

Almost as important is the quality of the publication's readership. If the sponsor sees that the audience you reach with your article is tightly targeted and closely matches the product, he or she is more likely to help you even if the circulation of the publication is small. For example, you may be able to secure funds or equipment from a rock-climbing-helmet manufacturer for an

---

Public relations (PR) firms versus in-house public relations departments

Some companies evaluate sponsorship opportunities in-house while others hire public relations firms to screen and recommend projects that may be of value to the company. It's imperative you target your proposal to the correct people. A few phone calls to the company will let you know where to send your requests.

PR firms are generally easier to work with than in-house managers because they are completely focused on finding good-quality publicity for the company. These firms tend to think of a writer as an opportunity to justify the funds they are being paid to disburse, while in-house managers often have difficulty just trying to find the time to evaluate a potential writer and may not fully comprehend the value of what that writer can offer their company.

article appearing in a rock-climbing magazine with a circulation of only 30,000. The same manufacturer may be reluctant to sponsor your article if it is intended for a general circulation newspaper, even if it has a circulation of 100,000 readers.

Serious students of the sponsorship game make a note of when a sponsor's budget year end occurs. Sometimes just before year end, funds are still available and must be used up. Projects that would not have been given the nod earlier in the year can suddenly be back on the drawing board. This use-it or lose-it philosophy (where money not spent is removed from the following year's budget) is common in many companies and can be used to your advantage. The other side of the coin is that firms may have already exhausted their publicity budget by year end and have no ability to sponsor you regardless of the merits of your project. You may want to pursue sponsorship money at the beginning of a new year's budget to avoid this situation.

2. Gaining the trust of a potential sponsor

Gaining the trust of the person in charge of the budget is essential. Public relations (PR) managers are bombarded with proposals to spend their companys' money and they quickly become wary of grandiose ideas pushed by people who do not carry them out. Here are some pointers to follow to assure sponsors you are not going to take their money without producing results.

- Prepare a good biography (known as a "bio" in the trade) detailing what you have accomplished with your writing

- Include clippings of articles you have had published

- Submit a polished and professional-looking proposal that shows you pay attention to details

- Make several proposals to the same firm — don't give up the first, second, or third time your proposal is rejected

- Show PR managers you understand what their job is and what results they expect

- Help managers look good to their superiors by sending them clippings of everything you write about their company

- Highlight anything that particularly benefits their company and came about as a direct result of your article

Sponsorship procurement is an art you will need to master at some time, regardless of your chosen subject areas. You may want to put on a seminar (to make money or for the public exposure) and find a company to foot the bill, or you may want to expand your articles into a book and need research money to cover the cost of travel or of acquiring research material. As your career progresses, watch how other people do it and ask questions. Many sponsors are willing to tell you what they look for in sponsorship projects.

3. The proposal

Any request for sponsorship should take the form of a professional-looking, well-organized proposal. Occasionally, you can pitch your idea over the phone and get approval in principle but just about all companies want a written record of exactly what you plan to do.

Proposals must cogently answer several key questions for the sponsor. The sponsor will want to know the details of the article such as:

- its proposed length
- its theme
- the hook — what makes the project irresistible?
- the angle you plan to write from
- what publications you can count on to publish your article
- what other publications you plan to approach about publishing your article
- the circulation of each of these publications
- when you expect the article to be published (e.g., August edition or winter edition)
- a precise list of what you need from the sponsor

When you outline the publications you expect to publish your article, it is wise to include a copy of your assignment letter. An assignment letter is a letter of commitment by a publication to publish a specific article. Usually, it is addressed to you on the publication's letterhead and includes the terms of your agreement with the editor: the number of words in the article, a tentative or working title, and a brief description of what the article is about. Your payment terms may also be mentioned in the letter, but if you plan to use the letter to solicit financial or other support for research, ask the publication for a separate letter outlining your payment. This is a common and widely recognized request from writers. Your potential sponsor doesn't need to know how much you will be paid by the publication for your article.

Expert advice

When we talked to Neal Matthews, he had just been notified he'd won the Lowell Thomas Travel Journalism Silver Award for 1997 given by the Society of American Travel Writers Foundation for a story he wrote on Antarctica. Matthews is a contributing editor for *Boating and Travel Holiday* and has traveled all over the world to write adventure stories.

Here is what he had to say about writing adventure articles:

- Photographs are crucial. In fact, you may want to pitch your story from the point of view of a photograph or image. Try emphasizing within the first three sentences of your proposal that there are excellent picture or photograph possibilities.

- Finding the right editor to work with is very important for a sustained career. Luck does play a part in putting you in the right place at the right time, but your work habits will determine whether the relationship grows or founders.

- High-quality, accurate work is essential.

- Always submit your material early.

- Arranging trips is the most tedious and most frustrating part of the job.

- Before you accept any sponsorship funds or equipment, read about and understand the policy of your target publication regarding freebies.

- Knowledge of other languages is helpful.

Judi Lees, a freelance writer with over twenty years' experience, has contributed articles to *Chatelaine Travel, Holiday Maker,* and *Ski Canada.* Lees uses a variety of approaches when sending query letters to editors. In addition to communicating via phone and mail, she has concluded the entire marketing of an article with an editor via e-mail.

Her prescription for success in the adventure writing field:

- Branch out. Although Lees focuses on outdoor activities and soft adventure writing, she says one of the joys of freelancing is the variety of topics that she can cover.

- Everyone wants to feel they are adventurous. Soft adventure is trendy with the aging baby boomers so try writing to this audience.

- On every topic, she says: "Research voraciously, but when you start to hear the same facts being repeated, it's time to write!"

George Hobica, adventurer and adventure writer for *Travel and Leisure, Men's Health, Travel Holiday, Country Living,* and *Success Magazine,* is an advocate of pitching ideas over the phone. To become a successfully published writer, he gives the following advice:

- Anticipate deadlines. If you are running behind and are going to be late, tell your editor.

- Always take a fresh point of view.

- Contact the different departments of major magazines and cultivate each editor's trust by submitting timely, accurate short pieces.

- Break into the field by writing for small community papers.

- Be creative and logical about where you submit your articles. "Adventures with Your Pet" will sell much more quickly to a magazine aimed at pet owners than a traditional adventure article would.

- Don't forget to follow up with the publication after you have submitted your article.

Hobica sees a trend toward service-oriented, practical-advice articles and says roundup articles (e.g., twelve things you must know/do/see before you cook/travel to/eat at...) are especially in vogue.

Lori Todd, editor in chief of *Via Nova Destination Magazine* in Roundrock, Texas, gave us these rules to having your article accepted for publication:

- The idea must be fresh.

- Sample writing must be well written and well organized.

- No typos! She admits everyone makes mistakes but when she sees errors, she can't help but assume the sender isn't paying attention.

- SASE (self-addressed, stamped envelopes) are important. They indicate you mean business.

- Invest a dime in a pocket organizer, those colorful folders with a pocket on each side. It makes an editor's life easier if he or she can keep all your material in one place with his or her notes attached.

- Your style is crucial — it must match the magazine's general style. Always analyze the magazine's style before you submit a query letter.

6

The Business of Business Writing

Commerce is almost as fundamental to society as language. Since people first learned the advantages of bartering skills and goods, they have been driven to find new ways of maximizing the benefits of doing business. Luckily, that means an ever increasing number of opportunities for writers to do business with magazines specializing in commerce of one sort or another.

It's tempting to think of business writing as dry, dull, and even — dare we say — boring. This perspective, however, often has more to do with choosing to read or write about a business subject that doesn't match your personality or interests than with the nature of business writing itself. For example, the reason accountants are so much in demand is because most of us don't like bookkeeping (when was the last time you balanced your checkbook?). But to a financial wizard, balancing books, calculating tax, and analyzing financial statements are all games that are not only enjoyable but profitable as well. The same principle applies to business writing.

Today, writing about business goes far beyond writing about traditional occupations and professions. You could find yourself looking at market trends, profiling a successful franchise owner, or investigating an upstart company that has all its competitors sweating beneath their three-piece suits. Subjects as diverse as mergers, bankruptcies, technological advances, educational programs, and yes, even scandals, can be angled toward the business-writing marketplace.

There are two main types of business publications:

(a) *Consumer publications*. These are aimed at the general public and usually cover broad business topics. These articles tend to sport titles such as "Business in Bermuda" or "Home Business News." Articles usually cover many different aspects of business, often profiling companies and their owners.

(b) *Trade journals*. These are usually produced exclusively for one specific business or industry. The articles are narrowly focused on that industry and will relate directly to their target audience. Titles such as The Pet Dealer or Cleaning and Maintenance Management leave little doubt these are publications aimed squarely at people who are already in the business.

Business writing, while demanding, is perfect for writers who are always interested in learning about the latest innovations, trends, and discoveries. You may be interviewing a lawyer one day and touring an engineered lumber fabricator the next — and you'll be constantly expanding your knowledge as well as your network of contacts.

a. You don't need to be an expert

A big surprise to many first-time business writers is that you do not have to be a business expert to write about business; what you do have to be is curious and persistent. Bear in mind you are writing for a knowledgeable but not necessarily expert audience. The number one reason people read business magazines and the business section of their newspaper is to gain information they can't find elsewhere. If you have good research and interviewing skills, you can write about a subject you initially know very little about. As a bonus, you'll become something of an expert yourself.

b. Research thoroughly

Research skills are crucial in business writing, especially when you are tackling a subject you aren't already knowledgeable about. And some of the best places to find information are as near as your computer, library, or telephone.

Some research resources we have found useful include:

(a) *The Internet*. With the ever increasing amount of up-to-the-minute information available on the Internet, this tool is fast becoming one of the preferred research resources used by many business writers. With a minimal investment of time, you should be able to discover at least a dozen Web sites relevant to your article. Be sure to bookmark them for future reference and visit them on a regular basis so you remain up-to-date.

(b) *Newspapers and other magazines*. There's nothing wrong with searching for information in other publications. Just be aware you can't copy directly from other publications; the ugly name for copying is plagiarism, the polite name is copyright infringement. Whatever you call it, it can be an expensive mistake.

(c) *Professional organizations*. For almost every business imaginable, there is an associated professional organization. Many of these exist almost solely for the purpose of disseminating information about a given profession. If you're planning to write about a particular business, cultivate a relationship with the local chapter of its professional organization.

(d) *People currently in the business*. All three of us are great believers in the value of networking. As you write more and more for a particular business or industry, you'll find your circle of contacts is always expanding. This is one of the best places both to research your current article and to mine for new ideas. Most people are more than happy to talk with a writer who is professional in his or her approach. After all, being quoted or mentioned in an article that is read by everyone in the profession is a great PR boost for the interviewee as well.

(e) *Annual reports and other public information.* Depending on the subject, these publications can yield a wealth of information. You can usually get them by asking the company concerned to mail them to you.

(f) *Government and public agencies.* Departments of Vital Statistics, chambers of commerce, workers' compensation boards, and even institutions such as banks and insurance companies may all provide documentation worth collecting.

(g) *Libraries.* Don't forget about your local library. No, we aren't thinking of just the public library. There are also university libraries, government facilities, and libraries maintained by associations or trade organizations which often have a wealth of pertinent information. On rare occasions, you may be required to pay a minimal charge to use these facilities, but our experience has been if you're courteous and develop a good rapport with the librarians, these fees will often be waived.

The best place to start your research is usually to ask yourself who or what first comes to mind when you think about the subject you're going to write on.

If you aren't confident about your researching skills, read one or two of the many excellent books available on the subject. Have a look at the appendix as a starting point.

c. Accuracy equals survival

Don't be afraid to ask lots of questions. You may think you'll look foolish asking questions when you're talking with experts, but many will be more than happy to share their knowledge with someone who is genuinely interested. And you certainly will look foolish — and harm your relationship with the editor — if your article is inaccurate.

Be meticulous with facts and figures. The difference between 0.5 percent and 0.4 percent may seem small to you, but in certain industries it's the difference between solvency and bankruptcy. Likewise, you should always check and double check names, titles, and technical terms. Very little will destroy your relationship with a contact faster than referring to the chief executive officer as the manager or misspelling someone's name.

d. Be careful using acronyms

NASA, CAT scan, NAFTA, SWAK — we are constantly bombarded with acronyms. Every publication has its own guidelines for deciding when a company is so well known that the shortened form has become the name, but until you are familiar with these guidelines, be sure you spell all acronyms and abbreviations out in full the first time you use them no matter how obvious you think they are.

Also be aware that acronyms and abbreviations change from industry to industry. In electronics, TTL means transistor-transistor logic, which is quite different from its meaning in photography: through-the-lens. If you're in doubt, double check — again.

e. Be a joiner

If you constantly write about one type of business, consider joining the relevant professional association. Not only will this produce an endless source of new contacts, but it will also increase both your visibility and credibility as a business writer.

While business writing may appear to be slightly less glamorous than other kinds of writing, in reality it can be quite exciting. In the course of your career as a business writer, you may well find yourself hobnobbing with some of the important movers and shakers of the economic world. Our experience is these people are most often easy to interview, articulate, and frequently have a good sense of humor about the idiosyncrasies of speaking with "the Press."

Don't shy away from controversy, but be sure you report honestly and avoid tunnel vision. Try to ask everyone the most basic and the most controversial questions surrounding an issue. Even though the first ten people may say the same thing, there is usually an opposing viewpoint somewhere that is worth delving into in more detail.

Like spelling, it never hurts to check your facts and figures one last time before you send out your article.

Expert advice

"Know who the readers of a magazine are and query magazines appropriately," says Eve Lazarus, a freelance business writer with a long list of writing credits including the *Globe and Mail, Canadian Business, Investment Life,* and a variety of in-flight magazines. "This always sounds so obvious that I can't understand why so many new writers overlook it."

Lazarus stresses the importance of professionalism — delivering clean copy, on time, in the format required. "An editor is paying me to get my copy in on time," she says. "It's simply part of being a professional writer."

She also cautions writers to pay close attention to the rights they assign to a publication. "Some contracts are really brutal," she says. "Certainly when you're starting out, you'll do some things you wouldn't do once you're established, but you need to think carefully before signing away all rights no matter where you are in your career. If I'm going to sign away all rights, what they pay me has to make it worthwhile."

7

Crafts and Hobbies

Come on, admit it.

We're willing to bet you didn't think of sunken treasure when you read the title of this chapter. If you immediately thought of knitting, macramé, and funky little carnivals where the vendors wear beaded headbands and dance to folk music, you've probably got lots of company.

The good news is that craft and hobby magazines have come a long way from the days of mimeographed sheets filled with cryptic instructions for creating a multicolored, cuddly mohair bedjacket. Today's hobby magazines run the gamut from traditional crafts to antique collecting to electronics and video plus everything in between. And yes, there is at least one publication aimed at adventurers who list treasure hunting with a metal detector as their favorite pastime.

Here are just a few subjects you may not have realized are a part of this thriving genre of article writing:

- Antique weaponry
- Beer and wine making
- Beer-can sculpture
- Birding (everything from hawking to birdwatching to carrier pigeon racing)
- Chainsaw carving
- Converting hub caps to solar mirrors

- Gardening
- Genealogy
- Ham radio operating
- Model railroads
- Pop-bottle capliner collecting
- Treasure hunting
- UFO watching
- Video making

Within the crafts and hobbies market, there are two very broad categories of publications:

(a) *Publications for doers.* These publications require an endless supply of classic how-to pieces. Some readers will be searching for highly focused writing about a specific hobby subject — a subject that is usually reflected in the title of the publication. Magazines such as *Apartment Garden Designs* and *Quilting Today*, for example, leave little doubt about their content. Conversely, other readers will be interested in a broad range of crafts that are either low cost or quick to complete. The general purpose of all of these publications is to appeal to readers who want to create something themselves.

(b) *Publications for collectors.* It's sometimes said everyone collects something, and a quick look at the range of magazines devoted to collectors of all kinds gives an enormous boost of credibility to this theory.

a. Articles for doers

Writing for the craft and hobby market is one of the oldest, most well-known forms of how-to. Even better, according to many editors in the field, the relatively recent surge of interest in back-to-basics, do-it-yourself nostalgia has boosted demand for articles catering to craftspeople.

There are other social factors fueling today's craft market: parents looking for new ways to spend time with their kids away from the television; individuals trying to combat the commercialization of holidays such as Christmas and birthdays by giving home-crafted gifts; or those who are simply searching for a

For anything that has ever been made, there is probably a magazine devoted to people who collect it.

diversion from the stress of city living. Whatever the audience, there's a growing demand for craft and hobby articles. If you have an interest in crafts and hobbies, and are prepared to do some research, you can convert your interest into a steady income. The following are some suggestions from editors in the field.

1. Don't skimp on details

Writing step-by-step instructions requires concise and complete directions. Sounds simple, doesn't it? Yet many editors mention lack of complete details as the error they most often see.

Writing for the craft market is probably one of the few markets where more is often better than less. In fact, many editors say they would much rather edit out instructions they felt were unnecessary than have to fill in or guess at missing information. Although you may be afraid you're going into far too much detail, the rule is to include as much information as you can.

2. Include a list of materials needed

Just as a list of ingredients is crucial to a recipe, a list of everything needed to complete the project is crucial to a craft article. Once again, the emphasis should be placed squarely on the word "complete." It doesn't matter how small the amount, leaving an item off your materials list in an article is a good way to increase your supply of rejection slips from publishers.

You should present materials in order of their use.

One editor cites a case where a project required a single dot of black paint in the finishing process. The writer, however, did not include black paint in the materials list and it was easy to visualize a reader getting right to the final step before noticing the need for this item. This omission wouldn't be a terrible disaster if the craftsperson lived close to a paint store and it was early Tuesday afternoon. However, imagine the wails of despair if this oversight didn't surface until ten minutes before the project was to be presented by a ten-year-old child to his favorite grandmother at her eightieth birthday. No time to go to the store for black paint and no finished present for grandmother either — just one very, very unhappy ten year old.

3. Photos! Send me photos!

The fastest way to grab a craft editor's attention is to submit a good-quality photograph of the craft project. Good quality means in focus, close up, and in color. Don't expect anyone to get excited about a papier mâché Santa Claus if it's impossible to see whether his sleigh is being pulled by eight tiny reindeer or seven dwarves.

4. One illustration could make or break your article

To give the editor an accurate idea of your project's size, place a ruler next to it when you take the photograph.

Often a single diagram will enhance your article enough to make the difference between a sale and a rejection slip. Don't worry if all the drawing talent in your family was inherited by your fourth cousin twice removed — these sketches need only be artistic enough to clarify any particularly complex parts of the project. Most publications have in-house artists who can easily create a finished drawing from your rough work.

5. Follow the rules and guidelines

Most craft and hobby publications follow a specific format, so it's important to look at several back issues and read their guidelines thoroughly before proposing an idea. If an editor wants to see the materials on a separate page in a bulleted list, you're wasting everyone's time if you send two paragraphs of perfect prose explaining the materials needed.

6. Test

Many women's magazines as well as general readership publications have a quick crafts section that's often a great place for writers to break into the crafts and hobbies market.

Build the bird bath or knit the patterned sweater yourself based only on the instructions you've written in your article. Better yet, get someone else to. If the finished sweater has arms that hang down below your knees, you'd be well advised to double check and possibly fine tune your measurements and instructions.

b. Articles for collectors

Collectors of all sorts read crafts and hobbies publications. These readers lust after more knowledge about their chosen passion and are interested in many of the following topics:

- What's valuable and why
- What may become valuable in the future and why
- The best places for buying, selling, or trading collectables
- News and reviews from associations for collectors
- Techniques for repairing and preserving treasures

- New ideas for displaying collections
- Upcoming conventions and trade shows
- Insurance concerns
- Profiles of experts in the field
- Famous collections (both private and public)
- True stories of new discoveries

These readers are demanding. They tend to invest a great deal of time and often a great deal of money in their hobbies. They are looking for information that will not only increase their enjoyment of their hobby but will also help their investments grow. All the editors we spoke with advised writers to check and double check facts for accuracy and never, ever talk down to your audience.

If you have a love of crafting or collecting, the crafts and hobbies market may be the perfect place to develop your writing reputation. And take heart. If you love funky carnivals and beaded headbands, there are even writing opportunities for that market.

Expert advice

What's the most exciting moment at the offices of *Crafts 'n' Things*? "When I open a letter and see a really great photo," says Nona Piorkowski, editor. "We always ask for photos, but sometimes one arrives that just shouts out, 'This is a craft that will appeal to our readers.'"

In addition to being the editor of *Crafts 'n' Things,* Piorkowski runs seminars aimed at writers who want to break into the craft writing market. She says people are often surprised to discover that, in some ways, writing craft articles is similar to technical writing. "Because you must write step by step and in chronological order, it can actually be a bit dry," she says. "You must also do lots of double checking, especially when you make out your materials list."

She stresses the need to study a publication's guidelines closely in order to follow its stylistic requirements. "For example, we don't work with colored charts for cross stitch projects because our charts are printed on newsprint. Most publications want color, but we need black and white."

Piorkowski sees good times ahead for craft and hobby writers. "There's always been an interest in crafts," she says. "But now more people are going back to traditional crafts. They want to spend more time at home with their families."

8

Writing About the Food
We Love to Eat

Everybody loves food and some people think the next best thing to eating food is reading about it. A few minutes poking around in a large bookstore and peering at row after row of cookbooks will convince you the world is food crazy. If you include all the cookbooks put together by two friends over coffee, local fund-raising organizations, and mainstream publishers, books about food probably rank as one of the largest categories of books. In addition, nearly all mainstream newspapers have some kind of food section with recipes or discussions of food trends. And, of course, magazines devoted to food abound. Even many television programming guides contain a different recipe each week.

Food is certainly seen as entertainment. How else can you explain the abundance of cooking shows on television?

Food writing is glamorous. As an established food writer, you'll receive a constant stream of invitations to soirées where the very best food and wine are served. The people you'll meet at these events will often be sophisticated and interesting. As your reputation grows, you'll be invited to travel overseas on press trips designed to familiarize esteemed food writers with the newest restaurants, resorts, cooking schools, wine harvests, and vineyards. On trips like these, you'll be able to experience a behind-the-scenes view of how the business of food is conducted throughout the world.

There are many aspects of food to write about: restaurant critiquing, food trends, recipes in magazines and newspapers, recipes included in travel articles, recipes with wine selections, and dietary and health issues are just a few. Over time, you may find, like most food writers, that you focus on a favorite aspect of food.

a. Advancing your food-writing career

Here are some suggestions compiled from several well-known food writers that are guaranteed to advance your career, regardless of the area of food writing you pursue.

1. Specialize

All the writers we interviewed agreed that to stand out in the crowded world of food writing, you must know everything there is to know about one particular area of food. For example, if you are specializing in a regional cuisine, you should know the history and legends of the region in order to give your description of the dishes a particular significance.

2. Travel

Travel is a terrific way to learn about both new and traditional dishes of a particular place. As a food expert, you'll discover that many dishes have interesting regional variations. Travel also gives you another means of communicating with your readers. An article that contrasts a local chef's recipe with the original recipe of the native country will likely appeal to readers who have traveled to that country.

3. Create a picture

Writing about food has similarities with cooking itself. Start with a particular food, such as a good cut of beef, and add to it the taste, smell, sizzle, color, and texture that readers would experience if they were actually eating or cooking the meal. Conjure up images in your readers' minds of exactly what it is like to be at the table savoring the dish.

Even an experienced food writer cannot know everything about every different kind of food and cooking. It's important when you choose a specialty to also have general knowledge about your topic. If you specialize in Chinese food, for example, you should also know about the philosophy behind Chinese cooking. Balancing yin and yang for good health is very important to chefs creating meals for Chinese consumers, as is evident in their balanced presentation of a spicy course followed by a bland course followed by a spicy course. This depth of knowledge is essential for your credibility as a writer.

4. Take a cooking course

Whether you plan to write restaurant reviews or spring new recipes on an unsuspecting public, you should take a cooking course. This will provide you with basic food and recipe knowledge (so you know, for example, that a classic Caesar salad does not have bits of cheddar cheese or chopped ham in it). The art of writing about food is the art of discrimination and by having an intimate knowledge of ingredients and procedures, you can communicate the subtle nuances that make one dish terrific and another, fish food.

5. Practice, practice, practice

Food writing takes practice, and not just eating either. The more you write about food, the better you will become at conveying subtlety. It is equally important to practice cooking the recipes yourself. Sampling the dishes during the cooking process is, of course, mandatory.

6. Read about food

Most good food writers read voraciously. Writing about food requires more than the ability to taste. You need to communicate your discoveries to your readers. By studying other food writers, you not only keep up with the latest trends and increase your store of knowledge, you also learn how other food writers reach their readers.

7. Learn the procedure

If you are determined to write recipes, learn recipe development format. There are numerous books at the library about the methods used in developing recipes. Read them from cover to cover.

Precise directions are an absolute necessity. If you leave out the correct size of pan to use and provide vague or confusing instructions, you leave your readers frustrated with the results.

8. Learn to edit quickly

At some point, you will have to chop part of an article you have written. It is not uncommon for a publication to quite suddenly ask a writer to cut 300 words from the article because the publication has oversold space to advertisers. In anticipation of

Your writing style will mature over time, almost through a process of osmosis. When you read a particularly apt phrase, it can remain in your subconscious, touching off associated words or phrases you may later use in your own writing. Take note of how other writers organize their ideas. A time-honored trick is to try to copy the style (not the substance) of an author whose writing you admire. You will be surprised to find as you grow as a writer, your writing matures and you develop your own signature style that actually incorporates some of your favorite writers' best qualities.

this possibility, you might want to group the least important details of the article together in the same paragraph or groups of paragraphs. Then, if you are asked to cut, you can simply delete these paragraphs. Picking out a word or a phrase at a time can be tedious and often disrupts the flow and pacing of the original text.

For more advice on writing about food, read *Writing Cookbooks*, another title in the Self-Counsel Writing Series.

b. Disadvantages? You bet!

Believe it or not, there are downsides to writing about food.

1. New wardrobe

With a constant stream of tasty tidbits tantalizing your tongue, your togs tighten. You may need either a new wardrobe or a membership at the local gym.

2. You're never home

Your home life can certainly suffer as you get ahead in your career. Between the restaurant reviews, promotions for wine or food, invitations to tastings, cooking courses you wouldn't miss, and networking every good writer must do, staying at home becomes a rare event. Kasey Wilson, an established food writer, says she is usually out working more than half of the evenings in a given week. Add to that the inevitable last-minute rewrites and evening writing sessions and she finds she works as many as 200 nights each year plus many weekends.

c. Free food

Only about ten of the top publications in the United States still pay all the expenses for a writer to do serious restaurant research. When you're just starting out, there is almost no chance you will be published in these top circulation publications anyway, so you will need to approach restaurants yourself and ask them to sponsor your meal so you can write a article. Use these pointers in your approach.

(a) Think about the article you want to write and come up with a succinct sentence or two that will convey the essence of your article to a busy restaurant manager.

(b) Call the restaurant and ask for the name of the owner or manager to whom you should direct your request. "Dear Sir or Madam" indicates a lack of serious commitment on your part.

   If you are writing a simple review, it's easy enough to state that's what you are doing. If what you are attempting is more complicated, such as comparing the newest version of Asian fusion to the original home recipes, your description will be a little longer. However, letters should never be more than a page.

(c) Include the name of the publication you are writing for as well as information on the publication's circulation. Restaurant owners want to know who you will reach with your article, and whether it is the kind of publicity they want.

(d) Explain how the restaurant will be featured in your article.

(e) At the end of the letter, ask if it would be possible for the owner or manager to give you a complimentary meal so you may write about it. You must be straightforward in asking for what you want. We have found that the more upscale and affluent for restaurant is, the more generous managers are. They are accustomed to having writers review their food and understand the value of the publicity it generates. Small restaurants may be more reluctant. In these cases, you may have to approach a number of different restaurants.

   Sample 1 is a example of a letter to send to a restaurant owner or manager.

(f) Include your bio. (See chapter 22 for more information on bios.)

(g) Make a follow-up call to the owner or manager of the restaurant a few days after you have sent your request.

To speed things up, approach a restaurant owner by telephone. Once things are agreed on, mail or fax a letter of confirmation detailing the dates you will be there and, if possible, the type of menu items you would like to try. If the restaurant owner or manager has asked for clips of recent articles you have had published, include these with the confirmation letter.

SAMPLE 1

Letter of Request to a Restaurant

Freida Fulsome
895 Caloric Way
Littletown, XC 12897

August 14, 200-

Jan Michael
General Manager
Waterside House
95 Tasty Lane
Goodfoodsville, XD 34567

Dear Jan:

I am writing an exciting new series for the *SunShine Daily News* (circulation approximately 100,000) called "Dining with Your Loved One in the Sunny City." Each column is dedicated to a romantic dinner for two at a fine local restaurant and the columns will be published once a week for the next twelve weeks. As I strolled past the Waterside House recently, I thought it would be an excellent restaurant to profile in this column.

Would you host me for a complimentary dinner? I can arrange any day of the week that is convenient to you.

A confirmation letter from my editor outlining this project follows, along with my biography.
Sincerely,

Freida Fulsome

Enclosure

Writing magazine and newspaper articles

Many novice food writers cringe at the idea that, by accepting food, it will appear as if they are selling their opinion for the price of a meal. There are two important points to remember about this arrangement. First, unless you are extremely wealthy, you really don't have a choice. Very few writers can afford the research that might cost them several hundred dollars a week just to begin building a reputation as an interesting and timely restaurant writer.

Second, even if restaurant owners or managers know you are coming, there is very little they can do to cover up problems in their service, the dining room decor, or even the menu. They are not going to repaint or offer a training course to their servers, and they either already have a talented chef or they don't. Beyond concerted prayer, there is very little restaurant owners can do to make your experience any different from that of regular customers without it being obvious to everyone involved.

d. Your credibility

As a food critic, your reputation with your readers, other food writers, and editors hinges on your credibility. Although opinions are subjective, there is often some general agreement about what constitutes quality and what does not. For example, everyone agrees fresh vegetables are preferable to rotten ones. Once you step outside the extremes, however, there is room for differences of opinion. As long as you present your ideas and opinions in a fair manner so that readers will feel they might share your opinion, your credibility should remain intact.

Since many of your jobs will come through referrals from other writers who are too busy to take on the project or from editors who have read your work, it is imperative to have all the facts straight and to present your opinions well in your article. Nothing destroys a writer's credibility faster — especially in the eyes of his or her colleagues — than outright errors and mistakes.

Pressures abound for a critic. Owners of restaurants do not like bad reviews. You can expect to receive calls during your career from irate restaurateurs who genuinely believe they have been wronged, or from others who are simply trying to pressure you into writing a good review. At some point, you will face the challenge of writing a negative review of a restaurant after you have spent a wonderful evening with the charming owners. It is also difficult to be objective when you know the owners have spent their life savings pursuing their dream of opening their own restaurant and your review might hurt their business.

In many instances, out of simple self-preservation, the truth should be tempered with tact. Publishing an unfavorable review of a local hangout in a small town, no matter how well deserved, can result in problems you may not have imagined when you wrote the article. You may find yourself ostracized socially or in business as people take sides on the issue. You certainly may find yourself unwelcome in some of the restaurants in town.

It is up to you to set your own boundaries as to which criticisms you'll present in your article and which problems you will ignore. One very effective and widely used tactic is to open with positive comments at the beginning of the article and tackle the negative issues at the end. Some writers, expert at the backhanded compliment, will write several glowing paragraphs about the appetizers while barely mentioning the entrées. Readers are generally smart enough to draw their own conclusions while many restaurateurs are snared by the opening lines of praise.

Of course, you ultimately have the choice of deciding not to write about the restaurant at all. Watch to see how other writers handle these kinds of problems. If you use your common sense, you'll find a way of dealing with all these issues that is most comfortable for you.

As a member of the media, you may be privy to sensitive or confidential information. As time goes on and sources come to trust you, they will confide in you. In fact, just by being in the food industry, you will hear all kinds of rumors. You will know whose partnership is about to break up (perhaps before the other partners do), which chefs are thinking about leaving, which investors are about to lose their money, and which restaurateurs have personal problems. If you relay this information to others, you'll eventually find your sources are less willing to speak with you. Remember the old adage "If you haven't got something nice to say, shove in another canapé." (Okay, we made it up, but you get the idea.)

Expert advice

Award-winning journalist Barbara Gibbs Ostmann has over twenty years' experience writing about food for newspapers and magazines. For fifteen years, she was the food editor for the *Saint Louis Post Dispatch.* As food writer for a *New York Times* syndicate, her writing currently reaches over nine-hundred thousand readers. Gibbs Ostmann has coedited twelve cookbooks with over five million copies in print and is coauthor of *The Recipe Writer's Handbook,* a style manual for creating recipes for publication. She teaches writing and has contributed to magazines such as *Better Homes and Gardens* and *Mobil Travel Guide.*

As a food writer and an editor who buys pieces, Gibbs Ostmann suggests the following tips for good food writing:

- Nothing beats good-quality writing as your ticket to publication.

- Never miss a deadline.

- Be accurate. If there are typos in your cover letter, how many errors are there in the recipe you sent?

- You must be your best every time, regardless of the project. You never know whom your editor will speak to about you.

- Take suggestions and criticism well. Do exactly what the editor wants for rewrites, quickly. Your editor is on your side and wants you to look better.

- Take an editing course so you know what happens to your article after you submit it. This will change your view of your editor's job.

- Compare the copy you submitted line by line to the actual published copy of the article. You'll learn something about what the editor wants.

- Become familiar with the publication for which you are writing.

- Get the correct name of the editor to whom you are submitting. Call the publication's office to double check.

- Don't call newspapers or magazines or your editor on deadline days.
- Don't call an editor for continual hand-holding and reassurance. If your article was published, rest assured it was good. Your paycheck is the thanks you get.

Kasey Wilson is a freelance writer and broadcaster, editor of *Vancouver Best Places*, and author of several cookbooks. The Restaurant Association of British Columbia and the Yukon named her the Media Person of the Year for Outstanding Reporting in the field of Hospitality in 1996. Wilson's publication credits include *Northwest Best Places, Northwest Best Bargains, Zagat Survey, Seattle Weekly, Canadian Living,* and *Simply Seafood.* She has been featured on CNN, PBS, and NBC and cohosts a popular two-hour weekly radio show called "The Best of Food and Wine."

Here are Wilson's suggestions for submitting publishable articles about food:

- Specialize.
- Be true to yourself. All you have is your credibility.
- Educate yourself. Take courses in wine tasting and cooking.
- Start with small community publications. You are more likely to pick up credits there than at big national publications where you are competing with well-established writers.
- Be professional in appearance and behavior.
- Learn to be a good networker.
- Practice your craft. Write as much as you can.

Some major magazines want stories that are virtually impossible to do because the subject is too large to be properly covered in a magazine-length article. Or the editor may ask for what amounts to a small book proposal just to consider a topic. This may make the article uneconomical for you to pursue.
— Laura Daily

Laura Daily contributes to *Restaurant Business, National Geographic World, Boys Life,* and *Mountain Living,* among other publications. Here is her recipe for getting into print:

- Query letters should always be short — one page maximum.
- Daily finds obtaining work from query letters is increasingly difficult. She suggests instead that you first find an editor you can work with. Then always be consistent and reliable with that editor so he or she assigns articles to you on an ongoing basis.

9

Writing for Women's Magazines

From feminism to fundamentalism, women's magazines are a thriving part of the publishing industry, but it's a big mistake to lump all women's magazines together in one category. A quick glance at the racks of any magazine store will quickly produce magazines on every subject imaginable and geared to women of all ethnic and religious backgrounds, careers, economic situations, and leisure interests. If you want to break into this competitive and crowded marketplace, you'll have to target your articles carefully. *Bridal Guide* will have very different requirements than *Women Police*.

Here is a partial list of the types of magazines that fall into the broad classification of women's magazines:

- Beauty
- Bridal
- Career and working women
- Child care and parenting issues
- Diet and nutrition
- Fashion
- Fashion specifically for large or petite women

- Financial matters
- Personal relationships
- Romance and sexuality
- Social issues
- Sports, exercise, and fitness
- Weight control
- Women's rights

Writing for a national women's publication not only pays well but is a great addition to your bio. But, like most specific genres of article writing, there are some peculiarities to this market which you need to bear in mind.

a. Write about real people

Many editors and writers identify the need for articles about real people as an important trend in the women's publications market. Certainly there will always be stories about superstars and celebrities, but more and more publications want articles that talk about real people in the kind of situations to which readers can relate.

Your local newspaper is often a great place to find ideas for profiles of local heroes. When you find a great candidate for a profile, try pitching your story to some of the larger national publications that don't have the staff to hunt down stories from across the country.

This interest in real people provides numerous possibilities for article writers. First-person tales are gaining a loyal following while profiles of women in the community who have done or experienced something extraordinary have long been a favorite with both magazines and newspapers. The subjects of these articles are seldom superstars in the Hollywood sense but rather, women who have achieved something, be it on a local or national level. You will quickly realize the potential for an uplifting article about this local superstar.

b. Avoid stereotyping

Beware of underestimating the knowledge base and intelligence of the readers of the publication for which you are writing — especially concerning subjects that have, in the past, been regarded as for men only. Women are no longer willing to put up with the attitude that suggests there are any subjects or areas that are not appropriate for them. They want practical, informative articles to improve their minds and lives. If you believe women aren't capable of understanding things such as car mechanics and science, don't try writing for the women's market. Chapter 12 offers suggestions on keeping your writing bias-free.

c. Short is good

Short is good — that's word count, not size. Perhaps nowhere is the old adage "write tight" more necessary than in the women's market. Many women who are attempting to balance career, family, and personal life simply aren't willing (or able) to spend more than a few minutes reading an article, no matter how interesting or relevant. This presents a real challenge to writers who face shorter and shorter word counts for even the most complex subjects. Every word must serve a purpose by advancing the article or providing more information to the reader. So get rid of those cumbersome phrases like "in point of fact," and replace them with a word or words that are short, concise, and to the point — like "so."

d. Go for the unique

You've heard it before — over and over, in fact — "Give us something unique." In fact, by now you are probably cringing at the mere suggestion of attempting something unique.

Start by looking for what makes one publication different from its rivals. Perhaps it's a bridal magazine geared exclusively to second-time brides. Or maybe it's a Christian women's magazine with a feminist slant.

Now consider how that unique slant would affect your article. In the above two examples, consider the broad subject of raising children. Readers of the first magazine would probably be interested in an article about surviving the perils and foibles of blending families. But the same article geared to the second magazine will likely need an addition — perhaps how to teach Christian values. Regardless of your feelings about either second marriages or Christianity, you could produce an article which puts a different spin on the relatively common subject of blended families.

e. Time travelers need not apply

In most cases, women's magazines want current information that is relevant to today's woman whether she is a career professional, student, stay-at-home mom, married, single, or anything in between. Too many aspects of life are changing at too great a pace for your article to be anything but up-to-the-minute. Everything else is either nostalgia or ancient history.

f. Please press eight
to leave a message

Now that voice mail is an accepted part of business, you will find that almost all the major publications geared at women readers operate automated voice mail twenty-four hours a day. If you are contacting these publications by phone, don't expect to speak to a real person unless you've already worked with an editor and been given his or her direct line.

The market for articles geared toward women is huge and expanding. In addition to the plethora of women's magazines, more and more newspapers are now including a women's section in one or more of their editions. Pick your topic, find your angle, and you're on the road to breaking into this exciting and lucrative area of article writing.

Expert advice

"We are looking for stories about real women," says Maureen McFadden, deputy editor of *Woman's Day*. Except in cases of domestic violence or if there's a need to protect children, writers must be willing to use their subjects' real names and to submit photos of the subjects, says McFadden. "We aren't interested in talking about Alison Q. We want to know who the real person is."

McFadden's foremost piece of advice is to send for the publication's guidelines. "We update and change our guidelines all the time," she says. "So many people overlook the most important things. For example, you must, absolutely must, include an self-addressed, stamped envelope (SASE). If you don't, your query or article goes in the garbage because we simply don't have the staff to address that number of envelopes."

After you've read the guidelines, McFadden recommends doing some basic research and then trying to persuade her to consider your proposal. "Don't just say 'Hey, have you ever thought of a story about...?' Give me some concrete suggestions, a few sidebar ideas, and anything else you think would convince me there's a good reason to run your story."

McFadden also stresses the importance of reading several copies of any magazine to which you want to submit an article. "It's not just so you won't make a memorable blooper by submitting something totally inappropriate," she says. "Reading the magazine will help you frame new ideas. If you aren't getting ideas after you've read a magazine, it isn't the right one for you to be writing for."

Here are some of her other suggestions:

- Don't e-mail or fax your queries. Follow the standard rules of sending a SASE unless the publication's guidelines have indicated you can send your query in some other way.

- Keep the tone of your proposal professional, not chatty. "E-mail has just made a bad situation worse," McFadden says, "because it promotes an immediately informal, chatty style."

- Pay attention to correct submission format. Double space your manuscript and use plain paper. "You want the editor to remember you, but not for your spelling mistakes or the cover letter you sent on teddy bear stationery."

- Learn to research quickly and accurately.

- Learn to use the Internet.

- Back up all your material with reputable sources.

Luck can play a part in how fast your career grows. An article Susan Hauser wrote for the *Oregonian* was rejected. On a whim, she sent it to the *Wall Street Journal,* which not only published it, but began buying her submissions frequently. Various other publications saw her articles, which are pithy and conversational, and contacted her. Hauser has now written for *People, New York Times, Sunset, Los Angeles Times, Good Housekeeping,* and *Redbook,* all without having to market much. Of course, she did have previous writing experience, knew approximately what editors were looking for, and does write well, so luck may have pushed the opportunities to her, but she was ready and waiting with the right stuff.

Here is Hauser's list of suggestions for getting your career off to a fast start:

- Major magazines sometimes have so many hurdles, it isn't worth your time to pursue stories with them. On paper, it may seem they pay well for articles — up to a dollar a word or more. However, by the time you have sent samples, a detailed outline, and a lengthy proposal, as well as writing the actual article and incorporating several rounds of the editor's suggestions, the pay may not be very good at all.

- Canvas friends for article ideas. Hauser gets ideas from friends and offers a free lunch for their ideas she uses. Casual remarks and activities from daily life form the grist for her stories.

- In your query letter, spell out exactly what you will tell your readers paragraph by paragraph: "And then I will. And then I will." Keep your letter to one easy-to-read page.

- The first paragraphs of your story must be the best and most compelling of the article.

- When you are writing, always keep your readers in mind. Ask yourself, what do the readers want to know? Related to this suggestion, Hauser says her article writing technique is to write letters to her mother and then take the "Dear Mom" salutation off. Keep sentences short with no ponderous prose.

Part II

Putting It All Together —
From the Outline to the Last Line

10

So Many Ideas,
So Hard to Choose

Ideas for articles are everywhere. And yet, many people still ask, "Where do you writers come up with all your ideas?" The classic, if irreverent, cocktail party answer is, "I pay $9.95 to a pack of elves in a small town in Colorado and they send me ten new ideas each month in a plain brown envelope."

The truth is most writers pick up more ideas than they can possibly use simply by taking a bus ride, going to the supermarket, or chatting with friends and strangers. All it really takes is a sense of curiosity about the world and the ability to realize most people are just as fascinated by the things around them as you are.

Here are five simple suggestions to save you the $9.95.

a. Reacquaint yourself with the wonders of asking "Why?" and "What if...?"

While it sometimes helps to write about what you know, it is not always necessary. For many writers, part of the thrill of crafting an article is searching for the new information and personal contacts that are the result of the research and writing about a subject that is new to you.

What is necessary to be a successful article writer is a lack of inhibition about asking yourself and others *why* things are the way they are or what would happen *if* a certain event occurred. Your friends and family may wonder why you've suddenly begun asking about the inner workings of a combustion engine or just how the bookshelf in the kids' room was built, but don't worry — with careful training, they'll not only get used to it, but may end up sending you interesting newspaper clippings for your files.

Do you think there's nothing in your life that would interest other people? Here's an exercise that will banish forever that common myth. (In fact, the premise that original ideas are everywhere has itself been the subject of countless articles.)

Make a list of all the things you do well or know a lot about — even those you think would not interest anyone else. Don't be shy; this isn't the time to be modest. If you're intimidated by the mere thought of making a list of your interests, here are some ideas to get you going:

- Hobbies
- Sports (whether you watch or play)
- Pets
- Children
- Jobs (from your first paper route up to today)
- Travel
- Family celebrations
- Family tragedies
- Your medical history
- Your favorite ways of saving money
- Your favorite types of clothing

Surprised by how many things are on your list? Now try making another list of things — this time from events in your day-to-day life — where you might find the spark of an article. Don't worry about whether you know anything about the subject or not — just think of places where ideas may be hiding. Here are some of the ideas that frequently come up in writing classes; we're betting you'll find many more:

(a) The seasons and how they affect our lives.

(b) Festivals and holidays. Think beyond Christmas or Hanukkah. What about the Ides of March? Or Lammas Eve when the Norse trickster Loki is honored?

(c) People you know who have done unusual things. Between us, it took less than three minutes to come up with the following:

   (i) Two people who, at the age of fifty-five, sold everything they owned to travel across Africa in a jeep

   (ii) A prim and proper high-school teacher who wears horn-rimmed glasses, long gray skirts, and her hair in a severe bun during the day, while at night, she works as a belly dancer at a Greek restaurant

   (iii) A teenager who belongs to an organization that conducts medieval jousts in authentic costumes

   (iv) A man who left his wife, had a sex change operation, and married the local chief of police

(d) Junk mail. Yes, you read it right. We all get it, most of us hate it, but there are often interesting tidbits of information to be mined from it. Fashion trends, business opportunities, and prices can all be found among these heaps of flyers and all can lead to article ideas.

(e) The evening news or morning newspaper. Where else can you find a more concentrated package of all the latest information about what's happening in your town or around the world? Sure, someone else has already written a piece on the subject, but you can bring a fresh outlook and new slant to any topic.

For example, to generate new ideas among students in her writing class, Susan uses an article about a lawyer who was convicted of embezzling almost a million dollars from the government but who avoided jail by pleading chronic fatigue syndrome had been the cause of his crime. The article was about the actual court case, but her students are often more interested in how he actually committed the theft, what the myths and realities of chronic fatigue syndrome are, what happened to the money, and what the lawyer is doing now than they are in the actual case. Any one of these related topics would make a great article that would be nothing like the original story. (Susan actually picked this article because, at the age of fifteen, she had her first romantic crush on this man — this revelation always brings a huge round of laughter in her classes but also immediately inspires ideas for several *other* articles!)

(f) Overheard conversations. There used to be a television program called *Kids Say the Darnedest Things*. If you've never spent time listening to the people around you in a restaurant, on the bus, or even in a public washroom, you're in for a treat when you discover people everywhere say the darnedest things. While we do recommend a modicum of discretion, eavesdropping anywhere, from parties to PTA meetings, often yields terrific results for the writer who keeps his or her ears open. And, as a bonus, in many cases, total strangers will be more than happy to explain their pet subjects in great detail to someone who is interested enough to ask a few questions.

(g) Your hometown. Become a tourist for a day right in your own hometown. We often forget every place on the face of the earth is a foreign, exciting destination to someone. Your good old hometown where you were born and raised can be a place of mystery and adventure to someone seeing it for the first time.

Head to a popular tourist spot or a place where people congregate, and eavesdrop as you walk down the street. Pretend you're seeing everything for the first time. Ask a lot of questions, even the typical tourist ones. Listen for foreign accents and languages around you. What brings out an "Oooh!" of excitement and what causes nothing beyond a blank look of disinterest? The surprises along the way could be your clues to potential stories.

(h) Organizations. Join a couple of organizations and, in addition to meeting new people and making new contacts, you'll be surprised how many saleable ideas will come out of the meetings. How about profiling the woman who is talking about a new trend in mutual funds? Or the man who has just launched a new line of pet food? Or the airline pilot who is about to be forced into early retirement?

If you keep your eyes and ears open, there are literally hundreds of stories waiting to be crafted from simply paying attention to the people and things that surround you every day.

b. Brainstorm for ideas

While it used to be considered trendy, brainstorming today has become recognized as a great tool for generating ideas. The subject can be as familiar as a favorite sweater and a warm blanket by a fireplace or as unfamiliar as the latest breakthrough in genetic engineering; either way, brainstorming helps open up unexpected avenues for any type of writing because it encourages fluid, creative, nonlinear thinking.

Many prestigious, high-profile corporations use brainstorming for problem solving. Think of yourself as joining ranks with members of the Fortune 500 group as you settle down to a rousing session of brainstorming.

Brainstorming (sometimes also known as webbing) is nothing more than encouraging your mind to play with and expand an idea. It works best with three or more people, but can certainly be done on your own. It's fun, always ends up producing at least one or two good laughs, and inevitably brings out so many ideas you'll stop wondering where to find ideas and start worrying about which ones you want to work on first.

We like to brainstorm when we're looking for new ideas to write about or when we can't decide exactly what part of a huge mound of research to single out for a specific article.

A number of years ago, Susan had just completed two grueling weeks of research on an article about real estate investment in a small, rural town. It had been an exciting two weeks because, unknown to her at the outset of the project, new legislation and government grants had just been announced which were about to have a very positive effect on the local economy.

And yet, when she sat down to write the article, to her horror, she discovered she couldn't get going. There was so much valuable and exciting information, she couldn't find a focus. A couple of hours passed by. She was still staring at a blank computer screen, although there was now a small stack of crumpled paper on the floor beside her — failed first drafts and opening lines which had produced some amazing gibberish but certainly nothing publishable.

Finally, she grabbed a blank sheet of paper and, after no more than five minutes of solid brainstorming, had realized there were two areas almost all of the people she'd interviewed had talked about — the waterfront condo development and the new hotel. Once she saw these two items could form the basis of her article, she developed a catchy lead in only a few minutes and, after that, the article all but wrote itself.

Everything is a potential idea. Don't question why keys and a car may suddenly make you think of a waterfall. Accept that they do, and allow your mind to pursue the new thought. Who knows where you'll end up?

Here are our best tips for effective brainstorming:

(a) Adopt an "anything goes, no censorship" attitude. No matter how unrelated, unusual, or out-and-out weird a thought might seem, there is no such thing as a good or bad response during a brainstorming exercise. One brainstorming session we recall started with spiritualism (thrown out as an opening topic by one of the students), progressed to travel in the Orient, then on to luxury health spas, and finally to some delightfully decadent ways of increasing the romance in your life (bubble baths, chocolate-dipped strawberries, and champagne figured prominently in this part of the discussion!).

(b) Don't use a computer to brainstorm. No matter how fast you can type, there is a different mental process and connection with handwritten words. A computer also makes it almost impossible to jump back and forth between topics as you think of other things. A computer forces you into a more linear thought process which is exactly what the exercise of brainstorming is designed to bypass or avoid entirely.

(c) Write as fast as you can; speed helps generate even more ideas.

(d) Put each word or thought in a circle or box instead of listing each one in a straight line, or below one another. It is much easier to expand an idea when all you need to do is draw a line, or a new circle, and write down the new thought. If you run out of room in the space where you're working, just draw a new line to a blank section of the page.

Figure 1 shows how one student brainstormed around the opening topic of cement and eventually came up with ideas about submarines and barbeques.

FIGURE 1

Brainstorming

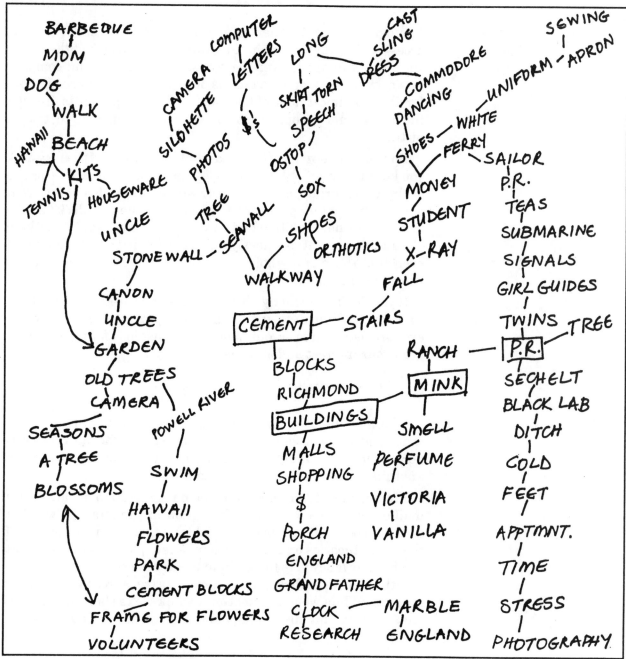

Reproduced courtesy of M. M. Brown.

So many ideas, so hard to choose

c. Remember writing is seeing, and seeing is writing

Photographs are another source of inspiration that is easy to access. Go through your photo album and take a look at the things you've photographed over the years. Don't worry about composition or whether you have dozens of pictures of the aunts in your family and almost none of the cousins. The purpose is to discover the things and people that interested you enough to take a picture.

Do you have dozens of before-and-after pictures of the new deck you built last year? Why not develop them into an article — or two or three? Naturally, a how-to piece would be one choice, but what about a lively story about the first party on the new deck? Or the impact your new addition had on your property taxes? What kind of building regulations does your municipality have? You might even find there is a whole new trend in building decks that is worth writing about.

If you don't have many photos or (like the three of us) you have so many it's difficult to know where to begin, you can also try this exercise using three or four magazines. Just look for pictures that grab your interest and start asking "Why?"

d. Be a voracious clipper

A clipping file is an invaluable resource when scrounging for writing ideas. Whether you do it while reading the daily newspaper or flipping through your junk mail, we recommend you clip anything and everything with potential.

From a short filler on a man who paid $2,000 in advance for a mail-order bride (never mind being left at the altar, he was left at the airport with no bride, no $2,000) to a detailed account of the latest theories on black holes in outer space — anything that catches our fancy gets tossed in to boxes under our desks. Once a month or so, we go through and sort these treasures into our filing cabinets. While we may sometimes think we're short on ideas, in fact, we've got hundreds ready and waiting at our fingertips.

e. Scribble wherever you go

You'll usually be able to pick out the writers in any group because they are the ones madly scribbling in tiny notebooks. Ideas can pop into your mind at the oddest moments, so keep a book with you at all times to capture your ideas before they disappear into the ether. If you see something that fascinates you, just jotting down a few words or phrases to yourself like "Collin, J-Showl, distr., shows" may remind you to pursue an idea that can be turned into an article. (Susan actually did convert these four words into a piece on art galleries which she then sold to a local business magazine.)

By now, you are hopefully brimming with ideas for articles, so it's time to put pen to paper and start writing. The next few chapters will take you through the process of planning your story — helping you avoid common writing pitfalls — right up to setting up your writing space.

11

The Elements of an Article

a. Outlines

The mere word "outline" strikes terror into the hearts of many new, and a surprising number of not-so-new, writers. Some writers blanch; some develop twitches or abruptly change the subject; many suppress a shudder or flat out say, "Oh, I don't need one of those. I have it all mapped out in my head."

But just as most people wouldn't dream of building a house without a set of blueprints to guide them, most professional writers don't begin a project without an outline to show them the direction in which they should be going.

There are a number of advantages to working with an outline.

An outline format is a fluid tool. Don't feel you must be restrained by a specific format for your outline — use whatever works for you.

(a) Outlines help you focus on exactly what your article is about. One of the most common errors many writers make is to try to cover absolutely every aspect of a topic — often in 1,200 words or less. An article about a rock group will be much stronger and more interesting to both your readers and your editor if it covers just the concert played in your city rather than if it tries to cover the concert, the band's history and future plans, and reviews of the band members' clothing, makeup, love lives, and past four world tours.

(b) An outline gives you a good idea of how long a particular writing project will take. If you know you need to write four sections of 1,500 words each to complete your outline, simply multiply the time it takes you to write 1,500 words by four, look at when your deadline is, and you'll be able to decide if you really can afford the time to go to that exciting new movie or all-night poker game.

(c) As you break a large writing project into smaller subsections, your outline does double duty as a checklist to make sure you haven't forgotten anything or repeated yourself.

(d) You never have to wonder what you're going to write about next, especially on those days when you're feeling less than inspired or would rather be eating the chocolate amaretto cheesecake than writing about it.

(e) If you need to make changes later to the order of the paragraphs so a piece sounds better, or to accommodate some fabulous, newly discovered piece of information, you will be able to see more clearly where those changes should be made by looking at the outline rather than at pages of the manuscript. The outline is the easiest place to make those changes. Once they're added to the outline, making changes in the manuscript itself is simple.

Creating a basic outline is much simpler than many people realize. There are only three essential elements: the same ingredients found in any good piece of writing. In most writing classes, when students are asked what the elements of any piece of writing are, they often try to avoid the question. Eventually, one student usually volunteers, "Beginning, middle, and end?" A ripple of laughter then goes through the classroom, indicating the rest of the class feels an outline could not be something so incredibly obvious. However, the laughter quickly subsides when everyone realizes these three items are the basics of any outline, no matter what the size or type of project.

Outlines aren't nearly as difficult as many people believe. They are an adaptable, nonjudgmental tool for you to use to plan and plot your article. In the same way that your writing reflects your individuality, your outline will reflect your personality and working style.

There really is no right or wrong way to create an outline. Rick likes to prepare detailed, formal outlines with subheadings and subcategories. Susan prefers a free-flowing form made up of ongoing notes jotted down at the end of her first draft; she then removes the notes as each point is covered in the article. Barbara uses a combination of both methods.

Many people find point form to be the easiest way of putting together an effective outline. The typical pattern is to spell out the basic topics and sections of the article and then expand and organize these into a larger, working whole. However, if you prefer to work with long, descriptive sentences right from the beginning, don't be intimidated — go with a style and format that suits your instincts and working habits.

As a rule of thumb, the more complex and longer your writing project, the more you need an outline. It will keep you on track, help you remember important items, and prevent you from getting lost in the various points you are making or the details you are describing.

b. Great beginnings — hook 'em fast

> Bianca Myddleton is the owner of Miss Milly House Cleaning Services Ltd. Her company is growing fast. It is almost three times as big as it was two years ago. She is thirty-four years old and has one child still living at home.

Has this opening succeeded in capturing your attention? Do you really care about who Bianca is or what she does? If you're like most readers and editors, the answer is likely "No!" Not only is this opening dull, but the string of short sentences make the passage choppy and uninviting. You've wasted forty-three words and said virtually nothing. Plus, the last sentence makes it unclear how many children Bianca has. Now let's look at the way Susan wrote the opening to this article as it actually appeared in an investment newspaper.

> Bianca Myddleton loves dirty houses. And understandably so. The thirty-four-year-old mother of one is founder, president, and franchisor of Miss Milly House Cleaning Services Ltd., whose company's gross revenues have nearly tripled from $0.5 million in 1995 to $1.2 million in 1997.

Both these examples use exactly the same number of words. The second example not only creates interest with an implied question (after all, how many people do you know who love dirty houses?) but also gives concrete facts about revenues, always an important issue to the readership of investment-oriented publications.

Most writers find crafting a strong lead the most difficult part of the writing process. And yet, the opening is your first and usually your only chance to make the sale to your audience. The impact of your opening will often determine whether or not the reader will continue to read. Whether your audience is an editor who may buy the article or someone just looking for some good Saturday morning reading, it's critical to capture your reader's interest immediately.

There is little leeway in the definition of "immediately." One editor we spoke to recently said if an author hasn't hooked her within the first three paragraphs, she puts the manuscript on the rejection pile. Another was more generous and said she would read two double-spaced pages before putting an uninteresting manuscript aside. By far the most common advice we have heard is, "Grab me in the first couple of sentences or forget it."

Many beginning writers complain this approach is cold, callous, and unfair. The truth is, it's simply a necessary business practice. If you walked into a furniture store and the first three sofas you looked at were falling apart, upholstered in hideous fabrics, or perhaps faded by sunshine and covered with dust, you'd probably make fast tracks for a different store *and* tell all your friends to avoid the first one. Because editors are in the business of buying quality manuscripts, they can't afford to spend their time poring over manuscripts that clearly don't fit their editorial requirements or are poorly written, any more than you would spend time looking at substandard sofas.

Here are two important things to keep in mind as you craft an opening to dazzle editors and readers.

(a) *Get to the point.* Your opening must give a clear and honest idea of what the article is about. A surefire way of turning off your editor and your readers is to open with a subject and then fail to develop it appropriately.

A classic example is the article that rambles on about how tulips are grown and then takes more than a page to get to the main point of the article — the just completed cultivation of a new variety. If you are writing a profile, be sure to name the person who is the subject early in the piece and be sure you identify exactly what the story is about before you launch into historical or other background information.

Here's how Susan began one profile article:

On March 21, 1993, Linda Williams was beaten, strangled, and finally suffocated in her own bed. The coroner estimated it took ten to fifteen minutes for her to die. She was thirty-one years old. Her killer? The man who ten years earlier had sworn to love and cherish her forever — her husband, Glenn Williams.

Right away, readers know who is involved, what happened, and why they should read this article. They also know they can expect an article with a powerful emotional impact.

(b) *Let your inner child out to play*. Get dramatic and passionate. Go for the sensual, the quirky, the ironic. Take whatever you believe is the single most fascinating part of what you are writing about and put it up front in your opening. Take a chance — if you allow yourself to be creative in writing your opening, it will make the rest of the piece that much easier to write. And, ultimately, if your gamble doesn't work, you can always go back and change things.

Spend as much time as you need to craft an opening that grabs readers' attention.

While some of the best openings defy definition (their originality is what makes them appealing), there are some broad categories of standard leads you can use. Understanding how and why they work will help you develop your own irresistible openings. One word of caution, though: Don't get so caught up in worrying about which type of opening you're going to use that you don't write one at all.

1. Use a relevant and interesting quotation

Quotations often provide interesting openings. Our offices have long shelves filled with books of quotations, from the well-known *Oxford Book of Quotations* to books with quotes about films, religion, food, witchcraft, inventors, and animals.

If you are writing an interview-style article, you may find a quote from the interviewee can make a wonderful opening. There may be a moment in the interview when it's as if the interviewee has just written the lead for you — a sparkling, clear moment that shouts "Ah ha! This is the opening." If this doesn't happen during the interview, try sitting with your eyes closed for a moment, thinking about the interview. What was your first thought after the interview was completed? What single thing struck you about the person you were speaking with? Exactly what did he or she say? The answers to these questions could easily provide excellent possibilities for your lead.

2. Use a takeoff of a well-known expression

There's an old joke that writers should "avoid clichés like the plague." But the writer who can twist words, sayings, and clichés can yield some clever, unusual openings.

One example from an unknown author says:

Money can't buy you happiness, but it can help you rent some.

Here's one from a student with a quick wit and a love of race cars:

Most people would give their eyeteeth to drive a formula one race car. Tell them to keep their teeth.

The article went on to describe a new facility where visitors and locals could experience firsthand the adrenaline rush of being behind the wheel of a race car.

As effective as takeoff openings can be, they can also be deadly. Be sure your takeoff is really funny before you use it. The acid test we use is to read the opening to an acquaintance; close friends and family tend to be too concerned about not hurting your feelings to be completely honest. If the acquaintance laughs, use it. If he or she gives you a pained or confused expression, head back to the computer.

3. Invite your readers to share your version of a universal experience

"Commuting. I confess, I can't stand it. Lineups, layovers, and the dreaded UFDs — unavoidable flight delays." Most people can relate on some level to the miseries and perils of commuting, so Susan used this as the opening for a review of a small Pacific Northwest commuter airline. Even though the article illustrated how none of these headaches applied to this particular airline, the opening gave readers the feeling they were being invited to share a common experience with the author.

4. Tell a story or anecdote

Story or anecdotal leads often make for strong openings. Nonfiction writers often forget that storytelling is part of human heritage and stories can play a part in nonfiction writing. Whether a story is fact or fiction, article writing can and should embody the creativity of storytelling.

> Klarissa thought she'd forgotten her ex-husband — the way he squinted his small dung-colored eyes, the small scar tucked along beside his long, sharp nose, and thug-like look he cultivated by ignoring his razor for days on end. She thought she'd forgotten the way his lips tasted of exotic spices and the passion his touch aroused in her body. She also thought she'd never see the inside of another emergency room. Last week, her broken nose and hemorrhaging kidney proved she was wrong — she hadn't forgotten any of it.

This dramatic opening sets the scene for a story about wife battering by recounting the true life drama of one woman. Notice how we know from the first sentence who the story is about, and from the first paragraph what the story is about.

5. Personify the main focus of your story

> She stood before me, wings outstretched in warm greeting. Her Plexiglas nose seemed to smile her pleasure at meeting me. "I'm glad you have come," she seemed to be saying. "It is good to see you."
>
> — *Manuel Erickson*

"She" is a World War II Lancaster bomber that now lives permanently in the Lancaster Museum located in Nanton, Alberta. The article continued on to discuss the history of the museum and its famous leading lady, as well as the community spirit and dedication of the Nanton volunteers. Personifying the subject of your story can be effective, if done well.

6. Ask a question

The purpose of opening with a question is to lure the reader (and hopefully the editor who will decide to buy your work) into the body of the article. A good question is one that immediately involves the reader in the outcome of the story. Make the reader believe the only way to discover the answer is by taking the time to read the material in front of them — your article.

There is, however, one major danger to this type of lead. There is a great temptation to pose a question which can be answered by a simple yes or no:

Have you ever wondered what it's like to fly a hang glider?

Not only are these usually flat, uninteresting questions, there is a very real danger that a reader, or an editor, will respond "No, and I don't really care if I ever *see* a hang glider, let alone fly one." When you use this type of lead, try to be shocking, controversial, emotional, or dramatic. And always aim for open-ended questions that create thought-provoking responses in your audience rather than monosyllabic replies.

Leads, whatever format you decide on, must intrigue your audience. Bait your hook firmly, then get set to reel them in.

c. The middle

We once heard of an informal study that claimed most novice writers spend approximately 80 percent of their time working on the middle of a writing project. The remaining 20 percent is split roughly half and half between the beginning and the ending.

On the surface, this makes sense. After all, the middle is the main course, the meat and potatoes of an article (or, as one politically correct and vegetarian writer pointed out, the rice and tofu) — all the facts and figures, development of the topic, arguments for and against, quotes, and historical data — in short, all the relevant details. Naturally, you'd want to spend most of your time working on this section. Right?

Not so. The same study revealed the majority of experienced writers actually reverse those percentages. Why? Because if you've done your job and written an opening with a great hook, your audience will probably continue reading the rest of your article no matter what. After all, they've invested a certain amount of time already, so they might as well finish the article. There are, however, a few noteworthy exceptions:

(a) *Poor writing*. The greatest hook in the world won't hold readers' attention through page after page of sloppy writing. We live in a fast-paced world where your words are competing not only against those written by others, but against television, the Internet, movies, and video games as well.

(b) *Misleading lead*. No matter what your subject, if your readers don't feel that you, as a writer, are delivering on your promises, they probably won't continue reading your article and may remember you as a writer to avoid in the future as well.

(c) *Inaccuracies*. Mistakes, even when they are honest ones, have a nasty habit of being remembered by the less forgiving title of lies. This is especially true when you are quoting a person in your article. The rule of thumb is: if you don't know for sure, either research until you are sure or leave it out altogether.

(d) *Superficiality*. While it may have been much prized by the pompous Gwendolen Fairfax in Oscar Wilde's *The Importance of Being Earnest*, superficiality is fatal to a nonfiction writer.

(e) *Offbeat presentation or grammar*. True, Jack Kerouac and e.e. cummings were able to flaunt their unusual style in the face of grammatical rules and get away with it. But until you are very well known, it's probably best to stick with normal, everyday punctuation, sentence structure, and paragraph format. There's a lot of truth in the old adage that claims you have to know what the rules are before you can afford to break them with impunity.

Make sure your manuscript is letter perfect. It never hurts to spell check one more time.

Before you start thinking you can afford to dash off the middle 1,000 words of your 1,200-word article on the joys of raising show dogs or how to build the perfect garden shed, here are some points to remember. Also, take a look at chapter 12, which covers some common writing pitfalls.

1. Less is often more

It happens in almost every writing class. Someone in the group turns out to be brimming with enough incredible stories and ideas that Scheherazade would have found herself with some very stiff competition for the sultan's attention.

Especially when you know a great deal about your subject or are particularly passionate about it, the temptation to include every minute detail can be irresistible. After all, you want to share all this marvelous information with your readers. Isn't that what writing is all about?

Well, yes...and no.

While 1,000 or 1,500 words may seem a daunting number to actually get down on paper, we guarantee that, in many cases, you'll find yourself wondering what on earth you can take out of your tightly crafted article which is now pushing 2,200 words. In a magazine or newspaper article, if you try to cover every aspect of a topic even briefly, you'll probably end up covering none of it well.

2. Maintain focus

Focus, a close relative of "less is more," is every bit as important to a writer as it is to a visual artist. If you've ever tried to watch an out-of-focus movie, you know how frustrating it can be. Is the riverside seduction taking place along the Thames or the Mississippi? And is that a rerun of *Planet of the Apes* or yet another sitcom about someone's perception of the in-laws?

Fuzzy focus will leave your readers confused, irritated, and ready to flip the page the next time they see an article sporting your byline. Let's look at an example:

> New Westminster is a city filled with antique stores and flowers. A large river winds its way past the public boardwalk where fish are brought in every day for the multitude of restaurants in the area. From Wild West to Asian, the area reflects the diverse background of its history and its residents although, recently, tension between different racial groups is increasing.

It's fairly easy to assume the article will be about the city of New Westminster. But exactly what aspect of New Westminster? Here are some possible focuses and the markets they imply:

(a) The buildings and ambiance of the city itself (travel)

(b) The restaurant industry (food: either a trade publication aimed at restaurant owners or a consumer publication with reviews of the food itself)

(c) Local history (historical or nostalgia)

(d) The racial conflict (political commentary, social sciences, or current affairs)

Each of these ideas is touched on in the example, but no focus has been defined in the article. Readers are left wondering what they should be expecting. Here's how one writer put together a well-focused concept for this piece:

> Sitting in the elbow of British Columbia's Fraser River, New Westminster is a grown-up frontier town paying homage to its pioneering past. Strolling the city's streets, I glimpse ghosts of the settlers' spirits: apparitions of horse-drawn buggies, swinging saloon doors, and weatherworn boardwalks mingle with the hustle and bustle of present day life.
>
> *— Kim Applegate*
> *(published in* Northwest Travel, *March/April 1997)*

We have a clear idea of the focus of this article — the intermingling of history with present day and how the past has influenced this city's present.

Now, how about a different view:

> Amid gaily painted fishing boats and posh restaurants, a time bomb is waiting to explode. Racial tensions are running high in New Westminster, British Columbia, where rival gangs of Asians and Mexicans have caused some residents to storm City Hall demanding increased police surveillance of the area.

This is obviously a fast-breaking political news piece. Even the tone of the article is different. The first version had a comfortable, easy-going tone that invited readers to take a stroll with the author. The second is hard hitting and to the point — here's the problem and here's what people want done about it.

And neither of these versions even touch on the antique stores or the restaurants. Those are two more articles just waiting to be written for other markets.

d. The ending

Like a good play or symphony, the best endings leave readers satisfied, yet longing for an encore. Remember though, the desire for an encore is very different from the sense that what you've told your readers is all you have to tell.

Summing up what was described is one commonly used and effective form of ending. Another is the circular ending. If you guessed this means referring back to something in the body of the article, give yourself a pat on the back; you're right. One student used this ending on a piece she had written about helping a child cope with his parents' divorce. She opened with the young boy asking how Santa Claus would find him this year because his mother and he had moved across the country to begin a new life. The article showed how his mother created new family traditions surrounding Christmas, and closed with the son, now a grown man, beginning to share those traditions when his own children asked how Santa always knows where everyone lives.

Aim to leave your readers with a sense of completion, and you'll soon develop an audience that can't wait to curl up in their favorite armchair with your next article.

e. Sidebars

Imagine being engrossed in an emotional article about the decline of panda bear cubs in China. You can feel the soft, black and white fur beneath your fingertips. A tear escapes your eye as you visualize the look of love passing between parent and cub. You're ready to hop on the next plane and join the fight to preserve these remarkable creatures now threatened with extinction.

Suddenly, an unexpected list of cold, hard statistics intrudes:

- number of panda reserves in China — 14
- decline in number of wild pandas worldwide during last ten years — approximately 50 percent
- number of times pandas have been successfully bred in China — 28
- fee charged by Chinese zoos to loan a panda for several months — up to $500,000

While this information adds important credibility to the work, the mood of the article has been shattered.

The solution? Put this information in a sidebar.

Sidebars are boxes usually run in the margin of the printed page containing information on anything from "How to Determine the Exact Number of Fleas that Can Dance on the Head of a Pin" to "Census Results for 1990 through 1995" to "Pros and Cons of Investing in a Fabulous Fellini's Franchise." They accompany many articles and are a standard way of inserting information that would otherwise break the flow of the article or destroy its mood. Readers can finish your article (or not) before they have to digest numbers, historical facts, instructions, or other less exciting information. Sidebars can also be used to effectively highlight important material in a quick information byte.

While it's impossible to learn everything about writing well from a single book, if you continue to practice, your writing will improve — guaranteed. Remember, like anything else, your creative muscle gets stronger the more you use it.

12

Gender Benders and Other Pitfalls

It would be impossible to teach stylistic points such as composition, imagery, and grammar in a single chapter, especially as there are so many good books devoted solely to these subjects (see the appendix). However, there are a number of common pitfalls to watch out for as you develop your craft.

a. Articles are a bias-free zone

Men or guys? Old folks or seniors? Jane Brown or Mrs. John Brown? Bias-free language continues to cause gray hairs and frayed tempers for both writers and editors. While taking this idea to ridiculous extremes is a party game played by some writers and editors (ever considered what the alternative to the term "manager" or the phrase "man your battle stations" might be?), the ability to produce bias-free writing is something you'll need to cultivate.

No matter how far we've come in the battle of the sexes, gender-based stereotyping can creep into the most unexpected nooks and crannies of your writing. Try to rid yourself of all the old misconceptions about how certain professions or positions in society are always held by either men or women. If your writing, even inadvertently, embodies these old clichés and stereotypes, you'll find it difficult to sell your articles in the majority of writing markets.

Some commercials use gender stereotyping to make their pitch more memorable. A number of years ago, one television commercial showed a woman woken out of a deep sleep by a midnight phone call. Shots of a jet warming up on the tarmac interspersed with the woman frantically pulling on her uniform, grabbing an overnight bag, and racing downstairs to hail a cab cued the audience to believe she's a flight attendant rushing to make a flight. In the final scene we see that, in fact, she's the pilot. This type of audience manipulation is frowned upon by most publications.

Gender biases are certainly not the only biases to watch for. Don't forget about biases related to:

- ethnic origins
- race
- age
- religion
- politics
- social status
- financial status
- profession
- educational level
- appearance
- weight
- physical ability

To help your writing remain bias-free, here are some options, ideas, and tips:

(a) Watch out for sexual stereotyping. For example, you'll seldom see a man described solely by the way he dresses, so avoid describing a woman in that way — unless you're writing a review of a fashion show.

(b) An increasing number of publications now favor the plural "their" instead of the singular "his or her" when referring to an unnamed person. While grammatical purists may wring their hands in despair, saying "A race car driver loves to show off their engine" rather than "A race car driver loves to show off his or her engine" is rapidly becoming the preferred phrasing in many magazines and newspapers.

If you are referring to a specific person rather than to a group of people, it is perfectly acceptable to use the appropriate personal pronoun: "Joe Speedy, well known race car driver, loves to show off his engine."

(c) Job descriptions pose another danger zone for writers. Gone are the days when you can refer to the post*man,* the fire*man,* or the house*wife.* First attempts to neutralize these demons of sexual bias were usually involved changing the offending suffix to person, e.g., postperson, chairperson.

A different option currently gaining popularity is to restructure the job title altogether; a stewardess becomes a flight attendant, a fireman becomes a fire fighter, a person who stays at home becomes a homemaker.

(d) Saying what one may do, one may experience, or one may learn is close to shooting oneself in one's foot. Using the pronoun "one" was once a common way of avoiding gender bias, but today it sounds awkward and will alienate both your readers and your editors. Try reading the sentence out loud — if it doesn't sound like something you'd say in conversation, try to make the tone more conversational.

The vast majority of magazines and newspapers do not like or use the "his or her" format for keeping articles gender neutral. Unlessthe publication specifies this format, avoid sentences such as "Each dog owner should ensure his or her dog is on a leash at all times." Not only does it sound a bit formal, it uses three words rather than one in a medium where space is almost always at a premium. Try instead, "Dog owners should ensure their dogs are on a leash at all times."

(e) Few women today appreciate being referred to by their husband's first name. If you write about Mrs. George Brown, for example, you can expect a call from your editor to find out what the woman's own first name is.

(f) Think challenged not disabled. Descriptions such as "mentally retarded" and "crippled" have long ago been replaced by ones like "mentally challenged" or "mobility challenged." This is an area of writing that is changing rapidly and you'll want to discuss any specific concerns you might have directly with your editor. As a general rule, if the term refers to anything that has ever been used to single out a group of people, proceed with caution.

In the end though, remember to be true to yourself and your own beliefs. Occasionally a publication's policy will be so restrictive, you may feel uncomfortable writing for it. Susan recalls two magazines, one which refused to print the term Christmas Tree, insisting it be referred to as a Season's Greetings Tree, and another large-circulation glossy that left her with the impression its all-male staff viewed women as cute, little baubles with no brains or abilities to do much beyond cook, clean, and produce babies. Her decision to withdraw her submissions was, in both cases, quite understandable. Remember that you always have the right to say no.

b. Get active — involve your readers

You'll read it in almost every writing book, and yes, you're about to read it in this one too. Active voice is better than passive voice. Why? Because it's more vigorous, concise, and involves the reader more than the passive voice does.

What is the active voice? It presents someone doing something in a direct fashion. In grammatical terms, the sentence's subject (noun) performs an action (verb) on an object. "The jury heard new evidence today" (active) is far more interesting a sentence than "New evidence was heard by the jury today" (passive). It's also 25 percent shorter.

The active voice puts the doer, the most important person in the sentence, right at the front so readers know immediately who is at the center of the story. A favorite example from an (unfortunately) undated clipping that lives in one of Susan's files suggests if the first line of Genesis had begun "In the beginning the heavens and the earth were created by God" (passive) rather than "In the beginning God created the heavens and the earth" (active), the Bible may never have attained its status as the largest bestseller of all time. While this may be a bit tongue-in-cheek, the active voice opening serves to bring God closer to the readers — exactly the purpose of this particular piece of writing.

c. Get rid of a lot of all those very useless words that really clutter up your writing

Writing articles is like sculpting. You begin with an idea and turn that idea into rough words on a page. Then you begin the process of fine-tuning and trimming words until there is no excess flab, no wasted modifiers or adverbs, just clean, precise prose. For most writers this is one of the toughest parts of the writing process. Take heart, it does get easier. Here are some tips to help you put your word count on a diet.

(a) Use a single descriptive verb instead of relying on adverbs. "He ran quickly" doesn't convey a vivid image of how the man was running. Instead, try these:

- He raced.
- He scurried.
- He galloped.
- He sprinted.
- He fled.

All the above give a far more accurate and interesting picture — the idea of someone scurrying away is quite different than someone who is galloping or fleeing.

(b) Get tough with your modifiers. Words like "nice," a "lot of," "many," and "pretty" say very little because they're vague and open to interpretation. After all, what's a lot of anything? If you love pizza, a lot of pizza would be a fresh, piping hot pizza delivered every night. Someone who can't stand pizza might consider one pizza dinner a year to be a lot.

(c) Forget the legalese. Stuffy verbiage is no longer fashionable even in legal documents and it certainly has no place in article writing. Here's a short list of a few common offenders and how to eliminate them from your writing.

Replace:	With:
at this point in time	now
enclosed please find herein	enclosed is
as a consequence of	because
in the event of	if
in addition to	and
a minimum of	at least

(d) Can you say it using fewer words? Whether you are writing an article, a poem, or a novel, you'll find first drafts can often be trimmed dramatically. For example, the third paragraph on passive voice above now reads, "The active voice puts..." but the original draft read "Another reason to use the active voice is because it presents..."

It takes time, but your ability to spot ways of trimming flab off your writing will improve the more you practice. Eventually, you'll find yourself automatically correcting sentences as soon as you write them.

Whenever you finish an article, use the find function on your computer to locate every instance of the word "that." In many cases, you'll be able to eliminate the word, tightening your article and making it more readable.

d. Building bridges is not just for bricklayers

Much the same as a bridge leads a traveler comfortably from one riverbank to the other, bridges made of words provide easy passage from one paragraph or subject to the next. A bridge can be a sentence or only a few words, but without it, your stories will sound choppy and harsh.

Here's an example from Susan's review of Holland America Line's ship *ms Nieuw Amsterdam*.

> A quick glance through the "Day at a Glance" bulletin assured me life aboard this grand lady of the Holland America Line would be an endless smorgasbord of indulgences for body and spirit. Massage, aerobics, ping pong, glacier watching, an art auction — where to begin?
>
> I decided to consider the question over afternoon tea in the Explorer's Lounge. Feeling oh-so-very-British, I sipped orange pekoe, nibbled delicately on crustless cucumber sandwiches, and admired the enormous oil painting of an ancient sea battle. Worldly cares seemed as far away as those billowing white sails.

The second paragraph could have begun: *One of my favorite activities was afternoon tea in the Explorer's Lounge.* This would technically have served as a bridge between the general list and a specific activity. But by adding only one extra word to the total count, a more lyrical, luxurious feeling that amplified the elegance associated with cruising was created. The writer was about to be so pampered, she could afford to take time to do nothing more than contemplate the choice of leisure activities.

e. Avoid subject hopping

Although too many different subjects create confusion and superficiality, most articles (with the exception of how-to articles) will include more than one. For example, if you are writing a profile on the latest pop singer, you will probably want to include a few steamy details on his or her love life.

As you re-read your finished masterpiece, you may get an uneasy sense of being out of focus, despite having paid careful attention to including only two or three well-chosen subjects. The problem may be subject hopping. Perhaps you've started with the singer's latest single that topped the charts earlier this year, then discussed his or her love life, then gone back to the single, then briefly discussed the backup band, returned to the love life, followed with more about the single, and wrapped up with a comment or two about the backup band.

A simple, effective method of seeing this problem is as near as a package of highlighters. First, take a yellow highlighter and mark everywhere you've referred to the singer's single. Now mark all the love-life details in green, and color every instance of how the backup band contributes in blue. Finally, use a pink highlighter for miscellaneous subjects.

Most well-written articles tend to display colors grouped together. If you're left with a frenzy of color that reminds you of the spinning lights in a discotheque, you need to do some restructuring.

f. Follow through

A common error among many writing students is to dangle a fascinating bit of information before the reader and then not follow through with it. Here's an example from one of Susan's classes:

> I finally found a motorcycle taxi and hailed it down.
> Getting on the tiny rear seat was a bit of an
> adventure because of my sprained ankle — but
> that's another story.

If it's another story, the writer should have left out any mention of it at all.

Here's a more subtle example:

> Small businesses are struggling. Companies that used to employ six people, now have only three; one that used to have fifty employees is down to twenty.

Did you catch the problem here? If you're going to say a company has cut its work force by 60 percent, many people will want to know the company to which you are referring. This sentence was rightfully cut before the article was published because the statement was too general.

Keep in mind language is constantly evolving and a publication's needs will evolve along with it. Our best advice is still to read thoroughly any publication you would like to write for and then call to ask for a copy of its guidelines, which should include stylistic requirements.

13

Point, Click, and Shoot

Why should a writer want or need to learn photography skills? Because articles will be much more saleable if they are accompanied by reasonable-quality pictures. To mangle a cliché, you can tell a 1,500-word story in 500 words if you have an evocative picture to go along with it.

Professional photographers, aficionados, and other fanatics will likely cringe at some of the advice in this chapter but, for the photographically challenged, it works. The key point to take away from this chapter is that you can take photographs without spending years perfecting the craft of becoming a photographer.

It's common to find photos taking up more space than the words. Editors know readers can be enticed to glance through dry statistics or instructions when a sizzling snapshot has already captured their attention, and your recipe will be much more evocative with a photo of the creamy goodness of your chocolate cake.

Every photo should tell the reader something extra or highlight a particular aspect of the story. Depending on the market, the photo doesn't have to be brilliantly composed or perfectly focused to tell its own tale. As an example, badly focused, grainy pictures of a flaming aircraft, taken from awkward angles, convey the terror of an air crash without having any technical merit at all. Photos like these sometimes sell entire newspapers and magazine issues regardless of the story text.

Even if you do not get paid for the photos, if your articles sell better with them, you're one step farther down the road to being a published writer.

While most of your photos won't have that kind of impact, if you follow this advice, you won't commit the sin of boring your audience either. Publishable photos really require only two things: some technical expertise and reasonable composition.

You can purchase just about all the technical know-how you need right in the camera. Good composition, on the other hand, is one of those intangibles you know when you see it, but is often hard to explain. But take heart, with practice and some attention to how other published photos look, you can develop a feel for good composition in a surprisingly short time. There are numerous books on photography available at any library. Spend a few hours studying them — the investment will pay off in short order.

The best part is that the practice is fun. Getting out there and using your camera is the easiest and most effective way to improve your photos. It costs a little for film and processing, but if you pay attention to what works and what doesn't, eventually you'll find your photographic stories becoming more and more memorable. And when your mother invites you over to show her some of your shots, you'll know the lessons are paying off.

a. Your first and only technical lesson

The syllabus for your first and only technical lesson is a bit abbreviated, but if you follow its secrets to the letter, you will be a technical expert. No shot will be out of focus, underexposed, or washed out by too much sunlight.

Step one: Go to the nearest camera store and buy a fully automatic camera. Auto flash, auto focus, auto film advance — auto everything. "Automatic" is a word the photographically challenged have come to love.

Sure, if you want to play with depth of field and f-stops you should be able to switch to manual mode, but with rare exceptions, you hardly ever need to adjust the settings to capture great shots. If you already know what f-stops are, you should skip on down to the section on selling your pictures.

Step two? There is no second step. With a modern camera, you are technically as good as many of the photographers whose photos are published today.

Shocking, yes. But you'd be amazed at the number of published photos taken with the cheapest automatic cameras.

Such cameras are not without limitations. Shooting just about anything except subjects eight or ten feet away means you lose all but the gross details. The good news is you'll probably seldom need panoramic shots for publication. Even if you do, there are dedicated inexpensive cameras that do panoramas almost as well as their more expensive counterparts.

b. Features to die for

So just what do all the automatic features mentioned above do? Auto focus lets you know ahead of time that every picture you shoot will be sharp. Auto exposure means every image will be correctly exposed. Auto flash means you won't have to make decisions about lighting in dim surroundings — the camera does it for you. Auto film advance allows you to take several pictures of a rapidly changing scene without removing your eye from the viewfinder. As well, many auto cameras also feature auto load and auto rewind, so when your last picture on the roll is taken, the camera rewinds the film.

These features may seem like costly bells and whistles, but in a one-chance-only situation, they can mean the difference between taking home a photo or just a memory.

Once, in Australia, when a little girl stuck her finger up the nose of a kangaroo at a petting zoo, Rick managed to be in the right place with his camera ready. Snap! A *Life* magazine back cover for sure. But the next second while he was manually advancing the film, the little girl turned toward the camera, and still holding her finger in the dazed kanga's nose, flashed a bedazzling smile right into the lens. Rick missed it.

When Rick finally had his prize photo developed, it was slightly out of focus and very dark. He had saved a hundred dollars by using an old manual camera and succeeded in losing his retirement jackpot.

On another occasion, he was photographing a skier doing some accidental death-defying somersaults, only to find afterward the camera had no film in it. The skier was not the good-natured sport Rick hoped he was and refused to do the stunt again.

c. Don't shop 'til you drop

Whether you are talking about an inexpensive pocket camera or a single lens reflex (SLR) with a variety of interchangeable lenses, there are at least a dozen camera brands to choose from.

Look for the most comfortable-to-use, fully automatic camera in the price range you can afford, and buy it.

When we finally investigated upgrading from our Canon Sureshot, we spent months reviewing dozens of different cameras — a whole new field with a lot of technical concepts and its own jargon. In the end, we realized all brand name cameras are just about the same. That's right. Any brand name camera will let you take good photos. Today's cameras and lenses are made by computer, so unless you are considering a camera costing under $20, any one of them will give you sharp, properly exposed images.

There is also a ready secondhand market. Not only can you save some cash when you buy your first camera, but when you are ready to upgrade, you can sell your "old faithful" and recover some of the cost of the new camera. But, just like buying a used car, it's smart to take along a knowledgeable friend and be wary of high-pressure salespersons.

d. In praise of disposables

Camera bugs may chirp in disgust, but disposable cameras do have their place. Picture quality, while not wonderful, is usually sufficient for most newspapers and many magazines.

There are also specialized disposable cameras. For example, unless you do a lot of underwater work for salvage or deep sea oil rig publications and can afford the big bucks to purchase or rent an underwater camera, the disposable underwater cameras are a very cheap alternative. They are good for photos down to a depth of approximately 6 feet (1.83 m) which is all you need for snorkeling, white water rafting, or swimming and boating shots.

Disposable cameras also make cheap backups for your normal battery-sucking, relatively fragile, main camera. Waiting for sunrise at the edge of a volcanic crater that took most of the night to reach is not the time to find out you have a malfunctioning camera and no backup. (Not that this ever happened to us, of course.)

Disposable cameras can also be used as a kind of currency. Barbara was shocked at the number of tourists who did not take a camera of any kind to the Great Barrier Reef in Australia. The boat crew on a tour she took produced a bag full of disposable cameras, which were generously offered to the passengers for about twice the going rate at the pier. There were several takers.

In really desperate circumstances, disposables can be worth much more. Rick graciously gave away his backup disposable to an unfortunate person whose camera died in the middle of a 38-foot (12 m) yacht race with some America's Cup sailors — a once-in-a-lifetime opportunity. Later that evening, a bottle of very good champagne was delivered to Rick's hotel room.

e. Lenses

Camera lenses come in three basic varieties: short, regular, and long; also known as wide-angle, normal, and telephoto. Lenses are specified in millimeters (mm) focal length. You can tell the difference between them first by their sizes. The wide-angle is short, the telephoto is long, and the normal lens somewhere in between. There is also a fourth variety, one which we recommend. If you can afford only one lens, go for a zoom. The zoom lens is by far the most versatile and combines various features of the other lenses.

Experts will tell you an assortment of the first three lenses will give you sharper photos than a zoom. Maybe. This advice reminds us of our first stereo systems. The salespeople talked us into much higher-priced systems because the sound quality was so much better. Frankly, Led Zeppelin sounded just fine on a cheaper system to us. Grainy newspaper reproduction doesn't get worse just because you used a zoom lens instead of the exact lens a professional might use. Today, even modestly priced zoom lenses outperform yesterday's models.

Choose the 35 mm to 70 mm zoom (or a 30 mm to 80 mm if you can get it). This lens is the best all-round bet, and you don't need to fiddle changing it for every shot. It rivals yesterday's normal lenses in sharpness and image quality at all settings, from wide (35 mm) to long (70 mm).

As well, most of these new, computer-designed lenses have a macro setting. In other words, they focus closer than other lenses, and at full zoom this means very close.

Just about every new SLR camera is sold with a version of this zoom as its prime lens, and for good reason. It combines versatility in a package hardly larger or heavier than a standard 50 mm lens.

Disadvantages of the 35 mm to 70 mm zoom lens are few, if any. For the very picky person who wants to use the slowest film, the lens needs a bit more light than a normal 50 mm lens. But if you use our recommended choice of 200 ASA color film, you will never notice.

f. Filters

Dozens of filters are on the market that do everything from polarizing light to darkening one half of the picture.

All you really need is a polarizing filter to cut down glare and increase contrast in brilliantly sunlit scenes. The best examples of the effect are those glossy travel magazine pictures of incredibly white sand with a deep turquoise ocean in the background. The filter is really useful at the beach or anywhere you are shooting a very bright blue sky or dazzling reflections.

Unfortunately, it is one of the most expensive filters on the market. And you'll need one for each lens unless your lenses happen to be all of the same diameter. Still, a polarizing lens works miracles in bright outdoor settings.

g. Film

We don't recommend using black-and-white film. Not only is it harder to find someone to develop it, you'll also want the option of selling the photo to color magazines, and increasingly, color newspapers. Besides, black-and-white prints can be made from color film, but without a good set of crayons, it's difficult to do it the other way around.

Some editors want color slides to work with. Others want prints. You need to know which before you purchase your film, since slide film is different from print film. It is possible to make slides from print film and vice versa, but the quality suffers dramatically and the processing is expensive.

If you are writing for a particular magazine, the submission guidelines will tell you which medium of image to submit. If there are no specific guidelines, submit prints. Prints are easier to handle, cheap to duplicate, and you don't need a projector or light table to examine them.

We recommend using 200 ASA color film. While 100 ASA will certainly do, 200 ASA allows you to shoot indoors, at twilight, and on dark and rainy days with better results. We also have had good luck with bulk or house brand film sold through large grocery or department stores. This film can be up to two-thirds cheaper than name brand film and for most applications it is just fine. The exception might be fashion or travel photography where color accuracy may be important. Try a few different films to become familiar with the differences.

One-hour processing outlets have improved dramatically over the past few years. We have had spotty luck with them in the past, but even local supermarket labs turn out excellent negatives these days. Developing through some of the large superstores can save you a bundle — up to 75 percent. Most cities also have several good custom labs. Ask around for a recommendation. A good lab should be able to correct minor exposure problems with your negatives by custom printing. Some can even take people out of a photo by digitizing it and using a nifty computer program.

Keep all your negatives and prints in a clean, dust- and moisture-free place that is not exposed to excesses of heat or cold. Negatives are best kept in an album with specially designed negative sleeves so, like prints, you can see what they are without fear of finger-prints or other handling marks. Sunlight fades colors, so avoid leaving negatives or prints where the sun might shine directly on them (e.g., on a windowsill). Treat negatives and prints like the valuable investment they are.

h. Before you leave home on any assignment, and on the road

Make sure your camera works before you leave home with it. If you haven't used it in a while, shoot a roll of film to make sure;

be sure to take flash pictures too. Trying to figure out what's wrong with your camera on the road can ruin a fun day. Finding out after you get home that your camera wasn't working is even worse.

Most cameras are too complicated for you to repair on the fly. Still, it is worth carrying a small repair kit with your camera. The emphasis should be on small. A basic repair kit includes —

- Super glue
- A few inches of duct tape
- A selection of suitable screwdrivers
- A small air brush for removing dust from the lens. This brush looks like a small turkey baster with a flexible bulb you can squeeze to force air through a tube — great for removing dust from fragile places.
- Silica gel packs to keep your equipment dry in humid places
- Spare, fresh batteries
- Your owner's manual

i.   The perfect picture

Composing a picture is the fun part of photography. The best way to learn composition is to go out and shoot pictures. Don't be afraid to waste film. Analyze your results; see how they stack up against pictures published in the glossy magazines. There really is no other way to learn the art.

Here are some suggestions which will help develop your inner eye.

1. Does the picture tell a story?

Imagine a cutline (caption) for the pictures you are taking. "Tinkersville is so poor the starving dogs all look like draped flour sacks." And, of course, the picture is of a pitiful-looking creature — all floppy skin and sad eyes.

The caption test is a good indication the photo may be unremarkable. If you can't think of an exciting cutline, the photo is probably boring.

2. Does the picture evoke an emotion?

People relate to other people in photos. If your article is about the love affairs in and around a county's bridges, a photo of fall leaves on a bridge deck might add a poignant dimension to the theme of your story.

A common type of picture is the close-up of a bevy of happy, contented faces. It may be cliché, but it turns up frequently because it shows the reader this is a marvelous place to eat, vacation, or gamble.

3. Does the picture show something unique or unusual?

One of the primary uses of a photo is to show the reader something out of the ordinary. Pick what you think is unique about a subject. Just be careful you don't pick something so "unique" it has already appeared in a hundred other articles.

Look for the unlikely. People are fascinated by unusual rock formations or ugly animals. These photos can be an arresting complement to your story.

4. What about people and animals as subjects?

People and animals are a safe bet as subjects for your photos. Put action in your shots by including people doing things — it gives readers something to relate to. Drinking coffee in an open-air café, riding a horse, swimming, and even shopping all draw readers into the scene. If people are not available, animals are good stand-ins.

However, both species should be treated with a bit of caution, for some have unexpected reactions to cameras which can make them dangerous. Rick once photographed a beach scene, only to have a nefarious-looking man break his camera for including him in the photo.

Animals and people also present another peculiar problem known as red eye. If all your relatives at the family reunion look like demons from *The Exorcist,* it might be the camera's fault rather than genetics.

Red eye is caused by the camera's flash reflecting back from the retina of the eye. The eye's iris constricts when faced with overwhelming light, but with the speedy electronic flash there isn't time for it to react. So the film gets an imprint of the entire vein system at the back of the eye.

There are several solutions. Ninety-nine percent of the time, this problem occurs when people are looking directly at the camera lens. Directing them to look slightly away from the camera usually avoids red eye pictures and, as a bonus, encourages a more candid aura to your shots.

5. Have you resisted temptation?

We are not alone in our attempts to imitate Ansel Adams's great landscapes. After many hundreds of dollars worth of wasted film, we learned the first commandment of landscape photography: stay away from all green-leafed jungle scenes, seascapes, and stunning panoramas.

Try to fill the frame with your subject. We once shot a whole roll of film of eagles with a pocket camera with no special lens. When developed, the photos were fields of blue sky with tiny dots in the center. Unless your subject fills at least half of the view-finder frame, get closer or use a telephoto lens.

The great panorama shot is always a temptation because there is a tendency to try to capture as much as you see. The camera, with its narrower field of view, cuts out most of it. Distant forest, star athletes, and most cities look the same all over the world and once you've seen one....

6. Where are the photos to be published?

When taking pictures to accompany your writing, consider where your photos are most likely to be published. Fine detail is often lost in newspaper reproductions, so get close and fill the frame with the subject (use your zoom lens).

Glossy color magazines require you to take more care to ensure the focus and exposure of the images are perfect. Don't send any that aren't.

Don't shoot pictures that require color for their best effect if you are selling to a black-and-white publication. This year's spring fashion colors will lose their glow in shades of gray.

j. Choosing photos to submit

If you managed to capture an armed robber on film just as he exited the bank, keep the words in the article to less than twenty. You can't do any better. But if your photos are not the central focus of your submission to a publication, pick out the ones you feel do the following:

(a) Supplement the story. One of Rick's stories about a small Mexican village marketplace was accompanied by a picture of a corroded Spanish cannon which two fishermen were trying to sell illegally to a tourist. The story said quaint, crafty, colorful things about the village while the photo added a dimension of skullduggery and mystery.

(b) Underscore a portion of the story or give readers an accurate view of something too complex to describe in words. Think of Dealey Plaza where J. F. Kennedy was shot and the relationship of the infamous grassy knoll to the School Book Depository. You could use a map and a bunch of words, but a photo from the right place explains it all.

(c) Show the reader how tall a basketball player really is or how broad the new hat brims are this fashion season.

When you are quite sure about what you want to underscore, select two or three photos to send with an article. Sometimes there are several points to a story, so you may want to send a representative sample of different subjects mentioned in the article and let the editor decide.

It is not unusual to have an editor call and ask if you have more pictures of a particular subject. The editor may have an idea what he or she would like to see but doesn't find it in the specific photos you sent.

Usually, you shouldn't need to send more than a dozen prints. Some writers send contact sheets (where negatives are printed directly on paper without being enlarged) to save money on postage and prints. This is especially thrifty if you are submitting ideas or queries to several publications at a time.

k. Submitting your photos

Never submit the negatives or the only print you have — especially if you are sending an unsolicited manuscript. If they get lost, it doesn't really matter whether it was the publication's or the post office's fault — they're still gone. One good option is to send color photocopy samples of your work. These are good enough for an editor to decide if your photos are useable, and if they go astray, you're out only the couple of dollars in copying charges.

When you do send photos, write your name and address, some information about the subject, and any appropriate caption on a small square of paper, and tape it to the back of each photo. Do not write directly on the back of a picture. It's all but impossible to press lightly enough so you don't score the front surface of the picture. Also, ink sometimes smears.

l. Other sources of photos

1. Trade associations and companies

Many trade associations and companies have spent thousands of dollars on professional photographs and have developed incredible collections.

Many of these companies and associations want publicity and seldom charge anything for using their photos as long as the article is about their industry or they get a mention. It is not uncommon to have them pay all shipping charges, which is especially wonderful when you are in a rush to meet a deadline.

2. Photo libraries and CD-ROMs

It used to be, in the old days before 1992, if you wanted a photo of a particular place or a particular subject and you didn't want to send someone out to shoot the picture, you could use a stock-photo library. All you did was reach for the photo library's catalogue on your shelf, thumb through the index brimming with any subject you could imagine, and then turn to the appropriate section for dozens of glorious photos.

Then you called the stock-photo office to find the price for a one-time or multiple use of a specific picture. Once you paid the price, sometimes several thousand dollars and rarely less than a hundred, you had your image.

With the advent of CD-ROM technology, multitudes of companies, such as Microsoft, are buying up entire libraries and reducing them to digital format. Now you can get several thousand images for $35, with often unlimited free usage.

Using equally cheap software, you can view these images on your computer, pick the ones you like, and transfer the digitized image to disk ready for mailing to the publication.

Most publications can deal with this medium, but the technology is new enough that standards are still developing. Be sure you check with the editor about exactly what he or she needs if you are going to use a digital format. And be sure to carefully read your licensing agreement on the CD-ROM wrapper to see what you are allowed to do with the photos. Some licenses allow unlimited use while others are restricted to noncommercial applications only.

m. Obtaining permission to reproduce

1. Get permission in writing

Photos and other images are subject to copyright laws. Using a picture without someone's permission is a good way to get your quill, and your bankbook, permanently broken.

To avoid confusion and legal problems later, get all releases *in writing* for each picture you use. Trying to get permission quickly over the phone can be dangerous. Verbal descriptions sometimes work, but too often you may find you are talking about one photo and a company representative is thinking of another out of its collection. Faxing photos usually helps clarify exactly which picture is being discussed.

Permissions, and the ease of obtaining permissions, vary depending on the photos in question. Since trade associations want you to promote them, they are usually happy to give you written permission to use a particular photo. Some CD-ROM manufacturers give blanket permission to the user to use their photos.

Some publishers will have guidelines outlining what is expected. For instance, they might require you use a standard form their legal department wrote, or they might want to acquire the permissions themselves, and all you need to do is supply the name and address of the copyright holder. Be sure you understand exactly what they want.

Keep track of permissions by stapling a copy of the picture to the release and putting them all in one file.

2. Is the owner of the photograph the copyright holder?

This is a complicated point, but one that writers run into frequently — permission from the owner of the photograph doesn't necessarily mean you have permission from the copyright holder. For instance, a hotel may have a picture of the property on the cover of its brochure it has used for years. The manager signs a permission statement that says you can use it, no problem. However, there is every chance the actual copyright holder is the photographer, not the hotel. The photographer may have given permission to the hotel to use the picture only in a brochure, not for publicity. Uh oh.

Your photo release form might keep you from losing a legal fight or it might not. Who wants to spend the time and money to find out? Be sure to ask who owns the copyright and who is licensed to grant permissions. Sample 2 shows a standard photo release form; you should use a form such as this before using a photo taken by someone else.

When dealing with small- to medium-sized bureaucracies, it's sometimes difficult to figure out who actually owns the copyright to a photograph. As a rule, the bigger the organization, the easier it is. Large companies can afford an art department which keeps track of who owns what and can quickly tell you if you can have permission to use a photo. In smaller companies, the person who arranged for the company to use the photo may have left without ever documenting fully who owns copyright. You can spend a lot of money and time trying to pin it down.

If there is a strong likelihood of your using a particular photo, find out as soon as you can who owns the copyright and what you are allowed to do with it.

SAMPLE 2
Photo Release Form

PHOTO RELEASE

Date: _____

I grant _____, and/or her/his legal representatives, the irrevocable right to reproduce the attached photographs. These images may be published for any professional purpose, including advertising. I will hold the above blameless from any liability caused by blurring, distortion, or alteration to the final photograph unless it can be proved the intent of such blurring, distortion, or alteration was to cause malicious damage.

I certify that I am authorized to grant this permission and that I hold the copyright to this material. I further certify that I have read and understand this release and consent to the terms and conditions as defined above.

Name (please print):_____

Address:_____

_____

Signature:_____

Witness:_____

NOTE: Be sure to check before you submit photo material to a publication to confirm this release is consistent with its guidelines. Some publications may require you to use their own release form.

3. Photographing people

Several points about photographing people are worth remembering. It is smart but not always practical to get the permission of the people you are photographing. A friend once took a photo of a man with a dancing bear in Turkey and then faced the choice of a beating or paying $10. The man made his living posing for tourists for cash. Everyone on the street except our friend understood the situation. Had he asked beforehand he would have known.

Also, you never know where your photo will end up. It is not unheard of to have the subject of photo recognize themselves in a publication and demand payment as a model. Ideally you want to get a signed release.

Sample 3 shows a model release form. The most important consideration for release forms is what releases the publication requires. These should be included in the publication's guidelines.

SAMPLE 3

Model Release Form

MODEL RELEASE

Date: _____

I grant _____, and/or his/her legal representatives, the irrevocable right to reproduce photographs taken of me on _____(date) at _____(location). These images may be published for any professional purpose, including advertising. I will hold the above-named photographer blameless from any liability caused by blurring, distortion, or alteration to the final photograph unless it can be proved the intent of such blurring, distortion, or alteration was to cause malicious damage to me. I certify I am over eighteen years of age and that I have read and understand the terms of this release.

Name (please print):_____

Address:_____

_____

Signature: _____

Witness:_____

Parental consent (if applicable)

I certify that I am the parent/legal guardian of the minor _____.

I have read and understand this release and consent to the terms and conditions as defined above.

Name (please print):_____

Address:_____

_____

Signature: _____

Witness:_____

NOTE: Legal age varies. Be sure you confirm the legal age where you are and have any necessary changes to the model release initialed by you, the model, and the model's parent/guardian if necessary.

14

I Was Going to Procrastinate Today, but I've Put It off Until Tomorrow

Ah. Procrastination. You'll hear it in many forms:

"I can only write when I'm in the mood."

"I'd love to be a food (business/lifestyles/gardening, etc.) writer, but I don't have the time."

"I've always wanted to be a writer, and that's exactly what I'm going to be just as soon as _____." Possibilities to fill in the blanks for this one include:

- I retire
- my spouse retires
- I get a good job
- I have my own space and my own computer
- I've redecorated my office
- my kids are in school
- my kids are in university
- my kids leave home
- I've finished the laundry and painted the house

Neglecting to place one's posterior on the chair to write is the biggest complaint among writers. Try sitting in your desk chair for fifteen minutes and write anything — such as a letter or the menu for next Saturday night's dinner — to loosen yourself up.

Any of this sound familiar? There are hundreds of reasons why people who say they want to write don't. Most of these stalling techniques are nothing more than procrastination caused by fear — fear of failure, fear of success, fear of the possibility of success. It takes real courage to sit down, pen in hand, or, if you're like the majority of writers today, in front of a keyboard, and just write.

But in addition to the fears, many people suffer from lack of organization of their time. There are probably hundreds of books on the market offering solutions to time management problems. Here are some of the ways we've found help us manage our writing time better. If your level of procrastination is extremely high, buy a book or take some courses to help you.

Keep in mind procrastination is self-correcting. Once you miss a few deadlines, you won't have any projects to procrastinate about. Published writers are not procrastinators.

a. Set realistic goals

Some professional writers assign themselves a certain number of hours each day during which they write — no phone calls, no laundry, no excuses. Others use total word count for the day as their measuring tape and may weed a bed of flowers or cook a batch of strawberry jam between the first and last word of the day. Some use a combination of the two depending on the project.

We tend to favor the words-per-day method because it makes it easier to plan. And the really good news is the numbers don't have to be so large they become terrifying. If you faithfully wrote only 500 words per day, Monday to Friday, you'd be pumping out somewhere between ten and fifteen average-length articles per month. In nine months, you'd have 90,000 words, or the first draft of a book-length project. And if you increased your commitment to seven days a week, that first draft would be ready in just over six months.

It doesn't really matter whether you choose one of these methods or another one altogether, a tiny step each day will eventually bring you to your goal. The important thing is to set goals you can live with but that will still lead you to your final destination of publication.

b. Avoid your personal time wasters

Identify your personal list of time wasters and then cut down on them. Here are some of ours:

    (a) Phone calls

    (b) Having a quick cup of tea and a muffin

    (c) Phone calls

    (d) Lusting after computer gadgets and gizmos

    (e) Unnecessary paper handling and filing

    (f) Phone calls

    (g) Sorting your in-basket for the tenth time

    (h) Reviewing notes/research for the twentieth time

    (i) Returning phone calls

Once we realized the phone was the single biggest time waster, we began setting aside chunks of time when we allowed our answering machines to do exactly what we bought them for — take messages. We usually turn off all the ringers when we do this, because a phone ringing is just too much of a temptation.

Everyone has his or her own time wasters: those things that seem so necessary, you simply can't imagine not doing them. Many of them, laundry for example, *are* necessary, just not for as long or as frequently as most people manage to convince themselves.

c. Break the project into manageable bites

We're the kind of people who like to see a lot of items checked off on our daily to-do lists, so we break tasks down into almost minuscule parts. Here's a typical example of a day's tasks as we approach the end of a short article:

    (a) Finish closing paragraph

    (b) Spell check

    (c) Polish writing

    (d) Confirm details for sidebar

    (e) Finalize sidebar

On those rare days when you simply don't get a lot written, give yourself permission to forego the guilty conscience. It will only make it harder to get back into writing the next day. As long as you remain aware of the difference between procrastinating and accepting there will, on occasion, be unexpected interruptions you can't avoid, you'll soon be producing more words with less trauma than you ever imagined.

I was going to procrastinate today...

(f) Print article

(g) Notify editor

(h) Courier to editor

If we'd just assigned the tasks of (a) Finish article and (b) Send to editor, we'd feel as though we'd accomplished less. We might also leave out a step such as that all-important final spell check.

If the sheer size of what you're working toward seems overwhelming, you probably need to break the goal into smaller pieces. Remember, the list is for you only. Do what works best in your case.

d. Writer's block

If you are blocked, or just not making good progress, try starting or polishing a different article altogether. Maybe you're working on a piece about small business machines. Take a break by spending an hour or two brainstorming a new piece about getting a child interested in gardening. When you use this approach, you'll return to the business machines article refreshed *and* feeling a sense of accomplishment about the 500 words you just wrote on the etiquette of handling gardening hoses for the under-six crowd.

Even tackling a different part of your current project can be an interlude that often yields some amazing results. Work on:

- a sidebar
- a chapter to fit one hundred pages from where you are now
- a chart or graph
- fact checking by telephone
- research for another project
- reducing your outline to another level
- anything to get your fingers flying over the keyboard again

e. The endless edit syndrome

Many would-be writers suffer from one insidious form of procrastination: the endless edit syndrome. These writers edit their work forever. It's never quite long enough or short enough or polished enough or…. In short, it's never perfect enough to send to an editor.

Does this sound like you? If you've been polishing your 1,500-word article on the mating habits of the French snail for more than a decade, set a deadline for the proposal or manuscript to be submitted, and stick to it. No matter how badly you *think* it reads, send your work out on the date you've set.

f. Take time out for yourself

If it makes you feel better, have a professional editor go over your writing before you submit it, but get your manuscript in the mail on time!

In addition to efficiently managing your writing time, take time to look after yourself. Writing may look like an easy task but believe it or not, a writing career has some health risks. Carpal tunnel repetitive strain syndrome, neck problems, and tendonitis are just a few of the painful and debilitating problems that can visit you. An inability to sleep can come with the pain, and tired, cranky writers are not productive writers.

Before experiencing any symptoms — tender wrists, shooting pain radiating from your elbow, and muscle cramps — you should take a few precautions. Once these symptoms start, they are difficult to cure and, especially in this business, have a tendency to get worse.

We find our writing is much more productive and goes more smoothly when we pay attention to our physical and mental health.

1. Get enough sleep and exercise, and remember to eat

No matter how busy we get or what the deadline is, we've learned from hard experience we need to get sleep, exercise, and food. It may be only a salad in front of the computer or a fifteen-minute walk around the park at the end of the street, but these things are essential to your health and therefore to your ability to write. Try the following tips:

(a) Stretch every hour. Stand up when you do — it forces you to move away from your computer or desk. Inhale and exhale deeply, and really allow your body to relax.

I was going to procrastinate today…

(b) At least three or four times a day, look out a window or step outside your door. Hold your hand approximately six inches in front of your face. Focus on your hand for three seconds. Now switch your focus to something as far away as possible — a tree on the horizon or the mountains or even a neighbor's house. Switch your focus back and forth several times to exercise your eye muscles.

(c) Your typewriter or keyboard should be level with your arms when they are bent 90 degrees from your body.

(d) To prevent neck problems, sit as straight as you can. This takes a bit of practice if you are prone to slouching, but it puts the least strain on your joints and muscles and increases your endurance. Check into the various back supports that attach to most office chairs if you have trouble with this.

(e) Your chair should be adjustable. At the very least you need to be able to change the height. It's better if you can adjust the back rest and slope of the seat as well. Since you will spend many hours in your chair, spend some money on a good one. Even if you can only afford secondhand, buy the very best you can afford.

(f) Many writers say propping their feet up six inches or so off the floor is helpful. There are foot rests available for this, but at $35 and up, we prefer an old box or stack of magazines.

(g) Always have adequate lighting. If you get headaches frequently when working, try a different light source or move the one you have.

(h) Don't sit in a draft. Susan once found her back muscles going into spasm for no apparent reason. Eventually, she discovered that by moving her desk three feet to the right several days earlier, she had placed herself directly in front of the blast of cold air from an air conditioning unit. A simple return to her original spot and she was back in business and in comfort.

2. Indulge in a mini vacation — an hour, a day, a weekend

It can be as lavish as a weekend away with your best friend or as simple as a candlelight dinner, bubble bath, or a little quiet time with a trashy novel. A mini-vacation is about pampering yourself. So indulge and forget about writing for however long you've allowed yourself.

There will be times when all you want to do is throw your hands in the air and give up. The most important and worthwhile thing you can do for yourself on those days is to take a break.

Some writing instructors, such as Kenneth Atchity (author of *A Writer's Time*), even suggest faithfully making this time for play and pampering part of every project's work schedule. At the end of each segment, you know you'll be able to reward yourself for a job well done.

Whatever you do, take your body's warnings seriously. Don't give in to the old adage about how aspirin will make the pain go away. Masking pain now is a sure way to cripple your production later, and most writers don't have long-term disability insurance.

As long as you have other things in your life, you'll most often find you are able to come back to your writing feeling refreshed, inspired, and able to laugh at the inevitable rejection slips.

Take a break and do something you love — play tennis, walk along a beach with your dog, have a bubble bath by candlelight, go for lunch with your best friend, pick wildflowers in the forest.

I was going to procrastinate today...

15

A Room of Your Own

a. A quiet place

A pencil, a pad of paper, and, if you are human, an eraser, are all you need to start writing. Many writers get their start at the kitchen table, composing works of art on scraps of paper. For years, Rick had a small desk in the living room serving as his writing corner. With a good set of earplugs, it worked fairly well.

But making a living as a writer is more than just writing, as the rest of this book points out. Your kitchen table work space, pen, and paper will frustrate you and everyone in your family eventually. It won't frustrate an editor because few editors will agree to edit handwritten manuscripts. So before you are asked by your family to move into a hotel, consider spending a little time and money on some of the remedies suggested in this chapter. This is serious work, and you deserve to give it the best possible chance to succeed.

A separate office for your writing is not essential and not always possible. But no matter how cramped your home is, you must set aside some space to keep the business side of your writing organized. You might be able to take your writing out to the front porch, but not all the little things like staplers, paper clips, and mailing labels that go along with a concerted mailing campaign transport easily. Pulling everything out and putting it all away again can become a fatal obstacle to accomplishing even simple tasks.

Especially if you have children or a spouse, you will want a place where you can leave all your work accessible. Whenever you have a spare minute, you can address an envelope before you go back to laundry or dinner. If you can close a door, even better.

If you have an entire room you can call your own, you're lucky. Make your office as pleasant as you can. Aim for inspirational — whatever that may mean to you. You will be spending a lot of time there, so whether you like posters of exotic destinations or fantasy art or silk flowers on wicker fans, indulge yourself. It's your space; make it somewhere you like being.

Alternatively, rent a separate apartment as an office or join with a like-minded group of writers to split the rent for a cheery space. We've tried both of these strategies and, at the time, they were a scary expense to add to our tight budget. In the end though, our production rose dramatically and it paid off.

b. Communication tools

1. Telephone

One of your most important pieces of equipment is your telephone. Unlike fiction writing, where you'll rarely need a phone, you'll be using your phone frequently to track down and verify information when writing nonfiction. Using your own home telephone line is fine, just remember to answer calls in a straightforward, professional manner.

We prefer a separate line which we use only for business, and if you have a house full of teenagers, you will too. Call waiting helps if you have a single line for both personal and business calls, and it is cheaper than a second line. Just be sure your children know your calls take priority.

A phone extension in your office space is also a must. It causes confusion if you have to make your calls in another room. As a quick solution, use a very long cord if you have only one phone or invest in a cordless phone. You can pick up telephone extension cords at any electronics store.

You can use a simple phone with no bells and whistles, but we recommend a touch-tone phone with hold, redial, on-hook dialing, and a speaker phone. The speaker phone is essential. The first time you spend 20 minutes on hold using your head and shoulder to grip the phone, you'll wish you'd gone with the hands-free feature. You should pay no more than $160 for a speaker phone, and you can often find one on sale or at some of the discount stores for under $100.

2. Fax machine

You have two choices for your fax line: a dedicated line used exclusively by your fax machine or a single line that handles both phone and fax. In a pinch, a dedicated fax line can also be used for outgoing calls. So if you are waiting for a very important return call, you can still carry on with your research without tying up your regular phone line.

However, when you are starting out, you can make do without one. Just be sure your fax machine is near your regular phone so when you pick up the receiver and hear the warbling sound, you can start your fax without running to another room. Another option is to install a switcher to automatically differentiate between a fax tone and a regular phone call. These are readily available and cost just under $200.

Don't go overboard on a fancy fax machine. The extras we find consistently useful are a paper cutter, memory for when the paper runs out, and a document feeder. We also like the on-hook dialing feature.

You may want to incorporate your fax in your computer. Computer fax software requires little training to use, and the initial cost of approximately $100 will give you a modem as well (see section **e.** below for more on modems).

The drawback of computer faxes is that they are less flexible than a manual stand-alone fax. While you can receive faxes from any source, you can fax out only those documents that are created as a file in your computer. It's great for saving paper because you can preview and print only the faxes you want to have a hard copy of, but you won't be able to fax a signed letter (unless you have scanned your signature into your computer) or fax copies of magazine and newspaper articles to people. You also can't fax back a signed copy of your contract to write an article.

So, even with a fax/modem for your computer installed, you may still need a conventional fax machine.

3. Answering machine or service

Who answers the telephone while you are out? If you have spent the whole morning on the telephone trying to obtain information and have left countless messages on different voice mails, you can be sure everyone will call back the moment you walk out the door.

Basic office equipment:

- *desk or writing surface*
- *adjustable chair*
- *computer and printer*
- *good light source*
- *filing cabinet*
- *telephone and telephone directories*
- *daily appointment calendar*
- *stationery: pens, paper, envelopes, postage stamps, paperclips, stapler, file folders, one or two three-ring binders, sticky notes, fax paper, address labels*
- *good dictionary and thesaurus*
- *fax machine*

The easiest, most common solution is to buy an answering machine. You will miss a few calls because there are still people who are reluctant to leave messages, but overall, a recorded message is preferable to an endlessly ringing telephone. People want to call you once and pass on the information you requested, not phone you back a dozen times trying to reach you.

Voice mail and call-answer programs offered by most major telephone companies provide extra flexibility and have been steadily dropping in price over the past few years. In the long run, they may still be more expensive than a basic answering machine, but they are often better suited to business requirements.

If you are sharing your phone with others, you may want to use a voice mail system that allows callers to choose whom the message will be delivered to. That way, you won't have to worry about not receiving your messages in their entirety, or receiving them secondhand.

c. Photocopier

To save money initially, use your fax machine as a copier. Most fax machines come with a copy feature that is sufficient for simple copies.

Personal copiers are the next step up. They run $350 and higher. They tend to be slow and may handle a limited range of paper sizes, but they will likely be fine for most of your needs. Or have a look at machines that combine a fax, answering machine, photocopier, and laser printer. Basic models start at less than $1,000. Not only can this be a cost saving over buying four separate pieces of equipment, but the space-saving factor is a major bonus.

d. Computer equipment

1. Computers

Like any craftsperson or artist, you need to have the proper tools. A computer with laser printer and the appropriate software is standard now for any business. Computers can save hours of your

If you are using your home phone, remember to put a short, professional-sounding message on your machine. Nothing puts business callers off more than having to listen to endless music and a long, informal message before they can leave their message.

Secondhand, reconditioned, or obsolete photocopiers can be had at substantial savings. We don't recommend buying a service contract on a secondhand copier because they are expensive and, for small volume users, they are not good value. There are plenty of photocopier technicians out there who can help you if yours breaks down.

time spent drafting and re-editing an article to fit a particular publication's requirements. Although a computer will be the most expensive writing tool you have to buy, the time it will save you in the editing stages will make your investment well worthwhile. Although there are writers who still love the handwritten word on a yellow sheet of foolscap, there are not many magazine or newspaper editors who do.

When purchasing a computer, stay with industry standards. Any store clerk can tell you if a piece of computer equipment is based on a standard model. Name brand computer equipment still commands a bit of a premium you really don't need to pay. Clones are so good these days, you can feel quite safe purchasing them.

There are people who regularly discard their six-month-old computer equipment the minute something bigger, better, and faster comes on the market. This means there are some incredible deals on secondhand computers for those who are willing to spend an hour or two looking. Check out your local newspaper and signboards in libraries, universities, or coffee shops for advertisements. Used computers are cheap, often come with software already installed, and have had the bugs worked out by the previous owner. You may even be able to find an IBM XT computer or XT clone (a very early model of the home computer), which will give you all the basic editing capabilities for as little as $50. You will, however, have difficulty locating software for an older machine, so make sure you know what you're getting into before you buy.

Newer computers with more memory and larger hard drives use software that gives you many more options for laying out a snappy-looking proposal with graphics and different type faces. Unless you are going to be doing a lot of complex proposals or spending a lot of time on the Internet, a newer model computer may be unnecessary.

New equipment with a warranty does give most people peace of mind. We recommend avoiding service contracts, because they tend to duplicate the warranty coverage of a new machine. Some service contracts are so expensive, they amount to prepaying repairs you might need. Computer repair and service has become

If you consider yourself computer illiterate, check out the night school cour-ses in your area for basic training. Learn a basic word-processing program, such as Word or WordPerfect, and don't worry about anything else. The idea is to make your editing easier. Although it might be helpful, you don't have to learn all aspects of the computer, such as its operating system.

highly competitive, and unless you live in an unusually isolated area, you should be able to locate a good repair service in the Yellow Pages or ask friends for recommendations.

2. Dedicated word processors

Halfway between an old-fashioned typewriter and a computer, are dedicated word processors. They tend to look like large electronic typewriters and some even have small screens. Some are extremely inexpensive and allow you to do many of the same things a computerized word processor does.

A word of caution: Some of the older, cheap word-processing programs may not have a spell check and a spell checker is essential, especially if you are a rotten typist.

3. Software

We have used all kinds of word-processing software and we all have a favorite. However, we can recommend all the major word-processing programs since they all do the essentials. Even the very cheapest are a joy to us compared to writing with a pen and paper.

If you find yourself in need of invoices or form letters, you can design your own (called templates) on most word-processing programs. By creating your own templates, you can modify each form to suit your own needs and preferences.

4. Carry it with you

Laptop and notebook computers have put one of our dreams within reach. We now can sit in a beachside café and write, rather than always being cooped up in the office. It's great for a change of scene and wonderful for drawing inspiration from the vignettes of life passing by.

Before you rush out to buy either a laptop or a notebook, consider the purchase carefully. Both laptop and notebook computers are considerably more expensive than regular computers, and many people find the display and input devices (e.g., mouse and keyboard) awkward to use. But, you may find the compact size and portability the best choice for your office space.

We are biased toward computers since with one machine we can do accounting, word-processing, keep our telephone books, and a host of other things we like to use. However, dedicated word processors are slightly easier to learn, as you have to learn only word-processing commands.

e. Electronic communication

While e-mail and sending documents by modem is fast becoming the communication mode of choice among writers and editors, it is acceptable only once you have been asked to do so. E-mail is the computer equivalent of an answering machine. You can leave a message for someone on his or her e-mail, to be read at a convenient time. The difference is, on this "answering machine," you can leave entire manuscripts or pictures in addition to your message.

You can also transfer files and information electronically by modem (discussed below). This is a direct computer-to-computer transfer of data without using e-mail. Unlike e-mail, the recipient's computer does have to be turned on for you to send data. Not only is it useful for transferring finished articles instantaneously (no more worrying if the courier got it there on time), it is terrific for any kind of collaboration between editors and authors, or among coauthors. You can work on the document and then hand it back electronically without leaving your office. It's exactly like transferring data by disk, but much faster.

More and more publications now accept assigned articles by modem or e-mail. Some are reluctant to do it any other way. So if you are not computer literate and don't know e-mail from an elephant, your options as a writer are going to become narrower and narrower. If you want to be a regular contributor to a publication, you should start working on your electronic communication skills right now.

Both e-mail and electronic transfer require you to have a piece of computer equipment called a modem. An internal modem fits neatly inside your computer while an external modem sits outside the computer case on your desk. Both types work equally well, though an internal modem will cost less and today is usually included in the price of your computer.

You do not need to have fancy equipment to bring you into the twenty-first century. A modem that transmits at 33.6 kilobits per second costs under $60 new and less than $30 secondhand.

People love e-mail because it allows them to communicate with someone without going through the social chitchat of a telephone call. Like an answering machine, it also gives you some control over when you respond to requests. Some people swear it gives them greater periods of uninterrupted time than they used to have.

As modems and other communications equipment become faster, try to stay within a generation of the newest advances. The history of computers shows the generation of equipment that is becoming obsolete is still widely used but less sought after, and therefore, relatively cheap.

Having an e-mail address is rapidly becoming something expected of a professional in any area of writing. In fact, many people are beginning to prefer using e-mail to other forms of communication. Even though it is still considered impolite to e-mail an editor without a specific invitation to do so, if you have an e-mail address, be sure to include it on your business card and letterhead.

Although not the highest-speed model available, it will work for Internet research and sending your files to a publisher.

You will need to set up an e-mail account with a local service provider (see your Yellow Pages under "Internet" or visit any computer store) or one of the big international service providers. Most of these companies will entice you with some free hours and low rates for every hour you use. Shop around. Normally $15 a month buys you five to ten hours of online time, which is more than enough for e-mail.

Programs for e-mail are relatively easy to use and are getting more user-friendly all the time. If it all seems too much, contact your local school board or college about continuing education courses or hire a computer student to give you a few lessons.

16

Paper Blizzard

a. Getting information

No matter what you choose to write about, you'll want new and exciting information flowing to you on a regular basis.

If you are a business writer, you'll want to hear about the latest changes in the world of commerce and in the big businesses you are following. Restaurant critics and food writers want to hear about new restaurants, cookbooks, and food trends.

One essential way to start the flow of information is to get on the mailing lists from the public or media relations departments of the businesses you are interested in. Generally this is a very easy task, though you may be shuffled around a bit. People are usually quite happy to put you on their list but may ask you to mail or fax a letter with the request. Sample 4 illustrates how simple it is to make such as request by mail or by fax. Be sure to include your return address.

Once you've contacted companies and you have subscriptions to every publication related to your subject, you'll be receiving every news release, press release, and brochure available and then some.

Suddenly that cheerful soul who delivers your mail won't meet your eye any more. Those friendly exchanges are a thing of the past. Your letter carrier no longer has a upright bearing but a posture bent under the weight of a mail bag. Your fault.

SAMPLE 4

Request to Be Added to Media List

Jan Josephs
123 Media Avenue
Littlewood, GA 98765
Tel: (999) 731-5555
Fax: (999) 731-5556
e-mail: jj@jj.net.com

September 27, 200-

Michelle Lindsey
Business Company
333 Mini Street
Megatown, OK 12579

Dear Ms. Lindsey:

I am a freelance writer. Would you please add me to your media list so that I may receive your press releases and information packages?

My contact information is above. Thank you.

Sincerely,

Jan Josephs

Your letter carrier may gripe but he or she has it easy. It's *your* office that's overrun with paper. You've nowhere to sit. You can't find anything and the wonderful ocean view that enticed you to choose your home is completely obstructed by piles of unopened mail. What to do with all this stuff? What to file and what to keep?

Unfortunately, there's no simple answer. We know of a weekly columnist who limits the amount of information kept to a pile no higher than five inches. The rest is more or less randomly thrown out. We also know a writer who keeps everything that arrives at the office for possible use later.

Your decisions will be based on what you write about. If you're producing a weekly column, you'll frequently be searching for information to write about in spite of everything that arrives in the mail or via the fax machine. What you keep may also depend on your space and how much paper you can tolerate in your life.

Deciding what to keep will become easier with time. Really. At first we kept everything, but didn't want to use valuable filing cabinet space on items of doubtful value. So the pile ended up in a huge mound in the corner of the office, all because of our fear of throwing out something valuable. One day, after realizing we hadn't gone through the pile in a number of months, we ruthlessly threw the lot out. We didn't read any of it. Didn't sort it. We just shoveled it into recycling bags. We haven't missed anything.

You are the best person to decide what information you need to keep. At first you may feel more comfortable keeping more than you need, just in case.

b. Organize what you do keep

One summer while attending university, Barbara went to work as an office assistant. The person who was training her had a quirk about what could be written on file folders and how they should be used. Their labels had to be typed and the folders had to contain information that was going to be kept in the office for some time. As a result, this person had homeless piles of paper all over her desk because she hadn't yet made her way over to the typewriter to neatly type up a label. Periodically she put all these pieces of paper into a miscellaneous file and felt content that all was right with the world. Until she had to find something.

Don't follow this mode of organizing. Chances are you are the only person who will read your files, so feel free to scribble on the top of them anything that will identify their contents to you. And use those files freely. They are relatively cheap if you buy in bulk at an office supply superstore.

We don't even have miscellaneous files. If it is worth keeping, it's worth a file. If you doubt your ability to find such an item when needed, you may want to set up a card file to reference where the data is stored.

Use as many files as you need. If you are working on a project for only two days and it will make your life easier to use fifteen files during that time to keep yourself organized, what difference does it make? When you are finished the project, simply slap a new label over the old one and the file is ready to use again. What could be simpler?

What kind of two-day project could require fifteen files, you ask? You might be talking with a number of different Italian restaurants and want a separate file for each. You may want to have a file for information you have read and discarded. You may want a file just for your sidebar material. You get the picture.

c. Filing systems

Other useful tools for organizing your material are color-coded files and a file cabinet. We use a separate color for each project whether it is an article for immediate publication or research for an article. Anything that relates to the business of writing, such as business accounts, details on couriers, and banking, we put in the same colored file, which doesn't get used for anything else.

After many years of using business card holders on our desks, we have all recently converted to a computerized data base. It was a lot of work to convert, but what a joy to use. Along with every entry is a space for notes about telephone calls or other information. Although the limited number of free hours in our day makes for tedious work transcribing the notes into a computer after a telephone call, we never type notes into the computer while we are talking. The person with whom you are speaking will likely be able to hear you typing.

Many people today are corresponding exclusively by e-mail. Even if this is your preferred method, keep paper copies of your correspondence. You never know when you will need a written record of what was agreed on.

Don't take notes on your computer while talking on the phone. It's one thing to silently write furiously as someone is telling you things (perhaps things they shouldn't), it's another to let them know you are doing so by the clicking of your keys.

d. Computer files

As you are organizing your office, don't forget to use that very important tool, your computer. Word-processing programs allow you to organize your files by directories, which helps to break down your mass of data into workable parts. You might want to have a directory for invoices, one for letters to editors, and one for articles you are working on. You might want to call a directory Gardening in Hawaii, and use it to store all the work you are doing to promote the sale of an article: a letter to an editor, your research, and thank-you notes.

Back up your computer files on a regular basis. Daily is not too often.

No matter how you organize your computer, back up your files regularly. Once a day is not too often. Consider the possibility of having to redo your words of wisdom if your computer crashes, and it will be a terrific incentive to remember to do a backup.

And don't keep all your backups neatly piled beside your computer. Yes, you are protecting yourself against a system crash, but in case of fire or theft, you could still find yourself without a backup. We solve the problem by sending out backup disks to a friend for safe keeping on a regular basis. We sometimes even store them in our car — anything to move all our valuable work off the premises.

Some time ago there was an item on the news about a man who had his computer stolen. He had been doing scientific research for eight years and all his data had been lost in the break in. It took three typists five months to re-key the information from his hand-written field notes. We can only assume he didn't have a backup. Don't let it happen to you.

Store a disk that allows you to boot your computer with your backups. Windows and several other operating systems have the means to make a "system disk." Be sure to write-protect the disk by pulling the tabs on the side of the disk to the open position.

A system disk allows you to get back into your computer under certain circumstances without calling a repair technician. It doesn't repair your computer, but you might be able to sneak some data out of a crashed system and keep working. It is great insurance that has avoided potential disaster twice in our careers.

Also, use current antivirus software which can be purchased at any computer store. This software will help keep your files safe. This is especially important if you are accessing the Internet or swapping disks with other writers. Remember though to regularly update your antivirus software against new viruses. Most programs can be updated by downloading information from the manufacturer's Web site.

17

Writing in the Age of Cyberspace

The Internet began gaining a foothold in daily life in the early 1990s. By the mid-1990s, it was firmly entrenched. The information superhighway now runs straight through the living rooms of many North American homes and the front reception of almost all businesses.

The world of cyberspace changes from minute to minute. This book is not an attempt to explain the mechanics of this new phenomenon. Like most people who use the Internet, we haven't the faintest idea exactly how the Internet works. In the same way our cars either run or don't run when we turn the ignition on, we feel no pressing need to understand the how of the Internet — we're only interested in what it can do for us. For anyone who does want to understand how the Internet works, a steady stream of books and magazines is available.

This chapter looks at two areas where the Internet can be useful to writers: as a research tool and as a publishing venue.

a. The Internet — wonder tool or research nightmare?

Rick's first experience with Internet research was watching a computer guru pick a word (we think it was "fungus") at random from the dictionary, and in less than three minutes produce a list of reference material five pages long. While Rick was still making a futile attempt to shut his jaw and make his eyes retract back to their normal size, the guru apologized for having limited his search to university libraries located on the west coast of North America.

The sheer volume of information available through the Internet is both its greatest strength and its biggest weakness.

There are several joys to Internet research:

(a) No one knows if you're still in your pajamas. The Internet is open for business twenty-four hours a day, so it's ideal for night owls and early risers — just log on and you're ready to go.

(b) As long as you have access to a power supply, phone line, computer, and modem, you can do follow-up or spur-of-the-moment research. For example, if a contact has been able to set up an unexpected backstage tour of London's Globe Theatre, you may want to brush up on your Shakespearean history before arriving. An hour or less on the Internet should help you speak with "infinite variety" (*Antony and Cleopatra*) about the man who helped make "all the world's a stage" (*As You Like It*) a "household word" (*Henry the Fifth*).

(c) No matter how obscure the topic you want to research, chances are excellent there will be information on it somewhere.

Researching on Internet research also has its perils:

(a) You don't need to be an expert to be published on the Internet. From your teenage neighbor to the person who delivers your mail, anyone can put anything on the Internet and no one necessarily verifies the accuracy. Your toughest job may be to decide what on the Internet is accurate and what is not.

(b) Remember that to quote from Internet documents, you may need permission just like you would from another source (see chapter 23 for more on copyright). Many authors, newspapers, and magazines use Internet material without attribution or permission. However, if you do this, you run the risk of embarrassing yourself and facing expensive legal problems.

(c) Until you become experienced in narrowing your search, you may find you are overwhelmed by the volume of information available on the Internet. Often there is so much material available it's hard to know what to keep and what to discard.

(d) The Internet can be addictive. If you're a compulsive researcher, it's often easy to put off actually writing your article on favorite hot sauce recipes in favor of doing some more research. Since no one can ever find out everything there is to know about a subject, you have to learn when to say "I have enough information. Now I will sit down and write."

(e) It's easy to lose track of the amount of time you spend browsing the Internet. If your Internet server provides unlimited access, it doesn't matter if dinner time has come and gone, the rest of the family has watched three movies, and even the dog is asleep in bed before you finally turn off your computer. If, however, your server charges an hourly rate, you may find yourself facing a nasty surprise when the bill arrives.

b. Internet publishing

Whether you publish your article in an e-zine (a magazine published completely electronically on the World Wide Web) or create your own Web page to showcase your ideas, consider the following points before embarking on your new Internet project.

The pros of Internet publishing include the following:

(a) Your words will be seen by millions of people worldwide. There is a possibility someone from the other side of the world will read your work, decide he or she absolutely must publish your writing, and come knocking on your door with

Anyone who wants to pursue Internet publishing must keep up-to-the-minute with changes in the way electronic media works. The Internet is a fast-moving, fluctuating marketplace. But it is a marketplace in its infancy. If you are looking for excitement and a challenge that won't become stale, Internet publishing may be exactly what you're after.

a contract in hand. (This is not as farfetched as it sounds. It actually happened to Diana Gabaldon, a well-known historical romance writer.)

(b) You don't have to worry about postage, paper costs, or enclosing a stamped self-addressed envelope — just post your work in cyberspace and you're done.

(c) You will probably get prompt feedback from other Internet users about your writing. Some of it can be helpful in honing your writing skills.

(d) Both a pro and con of Internet publishing is you can update your material much more quickly than with printed formats. The benefit is you can insert new material almost instantly and make changes that keep the article fresh and up-to-date. The downside, as Rick and Barbara have found in providing content for a large Web site on travel, is your readers expect your content to be new all the time. In some cases you must be prepared to update your material or respond to questions two or three times a week. Be sure you know what is expected in any Internet writing job.

There are, of course, also cons to Internet publishing:

(a) It's almost impossible to find paying markets for an article published on the Internet because there is still no effective method for determining payment. Although there are a few magazines produced exclusively online (e.g., *Omni*), to date we have not heard of any publications that pay consistently and well.

(b) Copyright law has not caught up with the information superhighway. Lawyers and government regulatory boards are struggling to develop suitable and, more importantly, enforceable policies. There is currently no way to ensure your copyright has not been infringed once your work has been placed on the Internet. You just may have effectively sold all world rights for zero dollars. (See chapter 23 for more information on copyright.)

(c) Many publishers don't yet recognize this type of publishing as a valid credential since it is almost impossible to verify. Words can be plagiarized and modified until there is little or no resemblance to the original work.

Part III

Selling Your Article

18

How Much Can You Earn?

a. Magazines

Magazines pay anywhere from a few dollars to several thousands of dollars for stories. Obviously, rates differ from one magazine to another, but they also vary with the length of the piece or the department in which the article is featured. Most magazines pay by the word, although others may pay a flat rate for an article. Payment on an hourly rate is unusual.

Your past projects and credentials will influence your rate of pay. A recognized expert will always command a higher fee than an unknown or first-time writer. Naturally, too, senior (meaning, in the trade, older, more established, and profitable) national publications with hundreds of thousands of readers pay more than local papers.

The American Society of Journalists and Authors, the Periodical Writers Association of Canada, and many other writers' organizations listed in the appendix provide fee guidelines for magazine and newspaper writing.

b. Newspapers

Newspapers pay anywhere from nothing to $400 or $500 for an article of several hundred words. What they are willing to pay changes all the time. The vast majority of publications pay under $100 for a 500-word article.

There isn't a huge difference in the amount paid for an article by, for example, a business magazine and a food magazine. Usually the size of its circulation will have more impact on the amount a publication will pay.

The good news is that you are generally free to sell the same article to many different papers with little or no revisions. Most papers do not want a worldwide exclusive, but be sure to find out what rights they do want. (See chapter 23 to find out more about rights.)

c. Freebies

Money is not the only compensation you may get for writing an article. In addition to recognition, which may be a large part of the motivation for all your hard work, you can also count freebies as part of your payment. In areas such as food, adventure, and travel writing, you may be invited on free trips and given free food, wine, spirits, and clothing to use while you are researching your story.

Several issues arise from taking freebies:

(a) Some publications have stringent rules about accepting gifts from the subject of your article. Some of them will not accept articles if anything has been given free of charge to the writer. Other publications don't have guidelines at all. Be sure you know what your target magazine's policy is regarding freebies before you begin researching your article.

(b) Some readers tend to question a writer's integrity if he or she accepts freebies. There is no one to stop you from modifying your story to reflect the restaurant or tour operator in an undeservedly favorable light if you are given a freebie. However, if you do this often enough, readers and editors will catch on and you will find it harder to sell your articles. Remember, readers may act on your recommendations and you should therefore never falsely represent a restaurant or tour guiding company as providing an excellent meal or tour package if, in fact, it does not.

(c) In fields such as adventure, travel, and food and wine, there is no way you could possibly pay to sample the wares. Sampling many entrées and six or seven bottles of wine could easily cost you several hundred dollars. Likewise, kayaking in the Arctic would set you back thousands of dollars. By and large, most newspaper and magazine budgets are so tight they will not help pay your costs except in

Many writers joke that freebies are their main source of payment. They eat like kings while they are on research trips and survive on tea and toast at home. Many writers' wardrobes feature the logos of major hotels and restaurants on them.

extraordinary circumstances. Often, the only sensible thing to do is to accept help from a supplier when it is offered.

(d) Many writers suffer over the integrity issue. Our advice is to be true to yourself and don't worry about what other people may think. There will be times when you feel entirely comfortable accepting support and other times when it is clear the support is being given to influence your opinion and, therefore, the outcome of your article. Trust your judgment in all cases.

19

Strutting Your Stuff

This chapter will help set you on the path toward publication. While there are no big secrets or short cuts that will slice your time in unpublished purgatory in half, the simple fact is, if you think like a salesperson, pursue your dream in a businesslike fashion, and stick with it, you will end up a published writer.

To sell your articles, you must cultivate a set of skills and attitudes that have nothing to do with writing. Many people love to polish their prose almost indefinitely. They might write terrific pieces but refrain from selling their writing because they consider sales crass and commercial.

Ideally, you should have a specific audience in mind before you even touch the keyboard or pick up your pen. As you become more experienced, your knowledge base of what different magazines and newspapers publish will increase, and you'll automatically frame themes and hooks to fit particular publications.

For example, as you savor a lobster bisque in the latest trendy restaurant, you'll find yourself thinking "*Food First Magazine* loves articles about lavish food. I wonder if I could get an interview with the chef?" Or perhaps you arrive in your dentist's office to discover a soothing miniature waterfall has been added to the reception area. You may find your mind wandering back to the magazine article you just saw about alternative methods of stress reduction or the one about feng shui (the Chinese art of creating a harmonious living space). Or perhaps you're the type of person who immediately wonders how difficult it would be to build your own waterfall and could write a how-to article for an arts and crafts magazine.

The transformation from writer to writer-marketer is the turning point for all amateur writers. Every freelance writer must eventually realize he or she does not want to work as hard as is necessary to create a perfectly crafted manuscript without getting paid for it. The following sections provide you with some tips on starting to earn money from your articles.

a. Know what opportunities exist

In order to fully exploit the magazine and newspaper market, it is important to know where magazines and newspapers get their editorial content. There are three main sources.

1. In-house writers

Large magazines and newspapers have sections devoted strictly to one subject (e.g., sports, food, community events) which appear in every issue. The articles in these sections are usually produced by staff who can write on demand about a wide variety of subjects as the need arises.

2. Syndication companies

In addition to their in-house writers, most newspapers and an increasing number of magazines acquire editorial material from syndication companies. These companies provide stories that appear in dozens or even hundreds of publications across North America. The stories are well written, topical, and extremely easy to acquire — they can be downloaded electronically at predetermined prices. Unlike when working with a freelancer, there are no article-by-article negotiations to contend with and the cost is often as little as $5 per article.

For a writer, however, publishing your articles through a syndication can be more trouble than it's worth. The pay is often low and some syndication companies can be difficult to work with.

Editors who want to see a particular treatment of a subject are looking for something a little different, or want an exclusive story for their publications, usually have to look for another source — the freelancer writer.

3. Freelancers

Magazines and newspapers use a steady stream of quality freelance articles. We all write freelance articles for different newspapers and magazines. Barbara and Rick are also freelance columnists for a newspaper. In other words, they are not on staff at the newspaper and do not have any obligation to continue writing their column. By the same token, none of the publications they write for have any obligation to continue running their columns.

Susan is a freelance features writer. Her articles are usually assigned on an individual basis so she knows ahead of time she will be paid for what she writes, but the publications are not obligated to continue giving her assignments.

To write freelance, what you offer must be fresh, inexpensive, and usually exclusive in order to compete with staff writers and the all-but-free articles supplied by syndicates. To make your writing a worthwhile venture, you'll have to adopt some strategies to make the most of your research and writing efforts.

b. Know your market

There is really only one rule of marketing: Know thy market before submitting.

Perhaps because it sounds so straightforward, it's amazing how often this simple rule is overlooked. But as any experienced writer knows, the surest way to increase your supply of rejection slips is to submit an inappropriate article to a publisher.

For example, the magazine *Modern Bride* is not going to be a likely prospect for an article, however well written, on surviving a divorce. Your chances of selling an article titled "Abortion: Every Family's Right" to *Catholic Digest* are probably nonexistent. As offbeat as these examples sound, such misdirected submissions are common.

Granted, newspapers tend to have a broader audience, so it is harder to define their readership, but you will still benefit from reading this discussion focused on magazines even if you plan to target newspapers. All publications, whether a highly focused, quarterly magazine or a daily newspaper targeted at every resident in a major center, will have its own way of choosing the

If a magazine has a column made up of tidbits of practical suggestions, places to go, or small news items, see if you can write something to submit. Not only are these short writing projects that can be completed with a minimum of time and effort, but they can build your relationship with an editor. Once an editor knows of your reliability and writing ability, you may be in a more favorable position when longer pieces are needed. Even if the article is rejected, you have built a relationship with that editor who is more likely to give you pertinent feedback on what the article needs.

Small town and local newspapers are always looking for articles. The summer months are often when they are really scrambling for newsworthy article ideas because many of their in-house writers are on vacation. This may be an excellent time to pitch your ideas to them.

information it wants to present and its own way of presenting that information.

So how do you target likely publications? Read the magazine or newspaper before you submit. Reading past issues (even just one) is, without question, the best way to increase your chances with a particular publication. Sound simple? It is.

But remember, reading a publication with an eye to potential markets is a very different proposition than reading one strictly for pleasure or even information. You won't have the luxury of skipping over sections that seem uninteresting or not relevant to your own interests. You must read everything: masthead, bylines, sidebars, subscription information, even the advertisements. Every one of these components will give you valuable clues and insights into what the editors expect from the articles they choose to publish.

At this point in most writing classes, someone asks, "You don't really mean read all the advertising, do you? Ads are only another way for the magazine to make money. Why should I waste my time reading *them*? You should read them because ads are like signposts about the readership. Let's look at two hypothetical magazines and examine five ads out of each.

Ads in Magazine 1:

- Alfred Sung perfume
- Ethical Mutual Funds — the environmentally sound choice
- De Beers diamond necklace
- Holland America Cruise Line
- Mercedes Benz sports coupe

Take a moment to think about the implications of these advertisements. Your aim is to establish as much information as possible about the average reader of Magazine 1. Some of the questions you should be asking include:

- What is the probable age range?
- What about income level?
- What kind of work does the average reader do?
- What level of education has he or she attained?

- What is his or her main reason for reading this particular publication?

Here is a typical classroom profile. Remember this is an *average* picture of an *average* reader; there will be many exceptions.

Profile: *Magazine 1*

Most readers of Magazine 1 are forty-five years or older. They are career professionals, probably female, with a minimum of four years' university training. Disposable income is not a concern. These readers enjoy the finer things in life and are more than willing to pay for them, but their preference is for understated elegance rather than ostentatious display. If they have children (some choose not to), they have enough money to hire professional care for the children in order to make their own life easier. Entertaining is probably an essential part of their business lives with the emphasis once again on understated elegance. They may read the magazine to keep up to date with social and economical trends, who's who in their field, and new ideas for enhancing their social and professional image among their peers.

By now, some of you will be screaming, Sexist! Stereotyping! Not politically correct!

And you're right. But for the purposes of this exercise, it's not only okay, it's important to look for stereotypes. Advertisers know they must make every penny of their budget count, so they will be looking at various venues for promoting their products using exactly these criteria.

A peek inside the covers of Magazine 2 will help illustrate this point from another angle. Here we find ads for:

- Harley Davidson Motorcycles
- Labatt's Dark Ale
- Copenhagen Snuff
- A twelve-CD collection of country and western favorites
- A Franklin Mint precision model of a Mack Truck

This profile implies a totally different type of reader. Here's the typical profile of Magazine 2's readership.

Profile: Magazine 2

Most readers will be male, between the ages of twenty-five and forty-five. The majority will have little or no post-secondary education and will work at some kind of manual or unskilled labor. Many will be married, but if they aren't, they may often be perceived as a tough guy and a playboy. Money, while not necessarily tight, certainly doesn't flow with the abundance it does for Magazine 1's readers, although there will always be enough to go out with the boys — quite often. These readers like to work hard and play hard. Magazine 2's readers may read the magazine to look for new macho toys, events like car rallies or rodeos where they might meet other like-minded individuals, or for articles that point out the errors of the establishment.

Now ask yourself the following two questions:

(a) What is the likelihood of readers of Magazine 1 purchasing an article about how to save $100 each month on their grocery bills by clipping coupons?

(b) What is the likelihood of readers of Magazine 2 purchasing an article about where to find the best auctions worldwide for people who collect Fabergé eggs?

Many people are amazed by the amount of information this simple exercise yields. Without even looking at a publication's stories and features, you have already formulated a good idea of who reads it, and you can begin planning how to start writing an article specifically geared toward that readership.

The next step is to examine the rest of the magazine, section by section, so you can tighten your focus even further. Here are some specific questions you should ask as you begin analyzing a potential market for your writing.

If you are targeting newspapers, you should consider these questions as well, but remember, newspapers have a less tightly focused readership than magazines.

(a) What does the masthead say? Usually located on the first four or five pages of the magazine, the masthead lists the names of editors, contributors, and all other personnel associated with the magazine, as well as information about subscriptions and distribution.

Check the titles of the writers closely. If most of the feature articles are written by staff writers, the magazine may be difficult to break into as a freelancer. On the other hand, if there are few or no staff writers listed and each issue features different authors in the masthead, this is an indication the publication relies heavily on freelancers for its material. You may have found a gold mine for your writing.

(b) How long is the average feature article? Although we've heard of publications that routinely request contributions of 4,000 words and then cut them back to 2,000 words or less, our advice is to submit articles of approximately the same length as the other articles in the magazine. If most pieces run 1,000 to 1,200 words, find another market for your article of 4,000 words.

(c) What tone is reflected in most articles? Some publications want only the facts. Others prefer a casual style, along the lines of letters addressed to your grandmother. Some want first-person accounts, others are only interested in third person. Don't allow yourself to be lured into the trap of believing different is better when it comes to tone. Any knowledgeable editor knows his or her readers' decision to subscribe is based, in a large part, on the tone the magazine chooses to adopt.

(d) Are the stories geared to people with or without children? Life changes with children. Regardless of financial consid- erations, families, especially those with young children, have different needs and expectations than those with only two adults and perhaps a pet to consider.

(e) Which age group is the publication targeting? As with children, age plays a major role in what readers expect. Be aware, however, that this does not mean seniors are inac- tive compared to twenty year olds. Many seniors today are much fitter than their adult children. In addition, because they have many years of experience behind them, seniors

To quickly estimate word count, take a random sample of ten lines of text from the publication and count the number of words. Calculate the average number of words per line by dividing that number by ten, and then multiplying by the average number of lines per article.

are often quite discriminating and knowledgeable about a wide range of subjects.

(f) What types of illustrations accompany most articles? Are photos black and white or color? Is the publication lavishly illustrated, with few words, or is the text more prominent than the artwork? Fashion, food, and architecture magazines are three examples of publications that often rely more heavily on illustrations than words.

(g) Are there topics or issues the publication would be unlikely to publish? Remember Magazine 2? This magazine is unlikely to accept anything about trends in the stock market because its readers probably don't invest in stocks in the first place. Likewise, a publication geared toward hunters is not a suitable market for an in-depth analysis of the benefits of gun-control legislation.

(h) What topics have been covered recently? If the last two issues have covered weather-proofing your garden shed and building a patio extension, it's unlikely the editor will be interested in these two subjects for several months, possibly longer, unless it is a specialty magazine dedicated exclusively to these subjects. Keep in mind, these types of articles can be tied closely to the seasons — few people in North America plant a vegetable garden in November.

Most magazines plan their editorial content months in advance. The rule of thumb is the bigger the publication, the farther ahead it plans. Sometimes you will do all your homework, submit a scintillating idea you know is perfect for your target market, and still receive a polite rejection. Then you pick up the next issue and, to your horror, what do you discover? Someone else has written an article on exactly the same topic as yours. As tough as it may seem, congratulate yourself. You obviously targeted exactly the right publication, you were just a couple of months too late, something not even the most experienced writer can always predict.

(i) What themes recur? Researching this question doesn't mean you should avoid any topic similar to ones recently covered. If you discover in a general outdoors publication articles on the migration patterns of snow geese, the mating habits of puffins, and government regulations to protect the bald eagle in three consecutive issues, you know something important about the editor. This person loves birds.

How do you know this is the editor's personal preference and not the publication's main target? A tight focus would be reflected in the title or mission statement of the magazine. For example, *Field and Stream* is obviously a magazine about hunting and fishing; aspiring writers should know to submit articles about hunting and fishing. Similarly, a title such as *Air Adventures* provides a strong indication the magazine wants flying stories. However, editors, like everyone else, have personal favorites, and sometimes these preferences are apparent. In many publications, it's possible to see hints of what those favorites are and use them to your advantage.

Turning back to the example above, take your newfound knowledge about the editor's preference for birds and work up an article idea with a unique slant. Perhaps there's a small but intriguing bird sanctuary near your home. Or perhaps you know someone who rescues injured wild birds, nurses them back to health, and then releases them into the wild, and who would love to tell you some of his or her tales, perhaps supplying a few choice photos as well. Add in some current statistics about the number of injured birds that never make it, and you have a story you already know the editor will at least be interested in on a personal level. It's a rare person who won't give even a marginally closer look to something he or she really likes. Even if your piece isn't accepted, the editor is more likely to remember your name if you've sent in an article that touches him or her on a personal level.

Ideally, you should read the five or six most recent issues of any magazine you want to submit to from cover to cover. Check your local library and don't be afraid to ask if you don't see the magazine you're looking for. Libraries can often order publications from other branches if they don't carry it themselves.

If you've tried the libraries, asked all your friends, and even checked your doctor's office for a copy with no luck finding the magazine you want, write directly to the magazine for a sample issue.

When you're ordering a magazine from a different country, be aware of the differences in currency values, denominations, and symbols. Susan once sent a request to a UK publication and inadvertently put a dollar sign instead of a pound sterling sign in front of her Visa authorization. This meant a month's delay in getting the sample because the magazine had to write back to confirm she was really authorizing a £5 charge (at that time the equivalent of $12.50) to her Visa, rather than a $5 charge.

Many magazines will publish the rate for a sample issue, as well as a subscription, on the masthead. If not, a fairly good rule of thumb is to take the single-issue price and add 20 percent to cover the extra mailing cost and handling. Even if this amount isn't quite what a publication charges for a sample, there are very few that won't drop one in the mail after you've shown good faith in sending a check.

If you are planning to target newspapers, you are probably better off reading several recent issues to check for tone, style, and focus than you are asking for back issues.

Such painstaking inspection of a publication may seem like time wasted, but most editors cite writers' lack of understanding about the needs of the specific publication as the most common reason for sending rejections slips. If you take the time to understand a publication's needs, you are presenting yourself as a writer with a professional attitude.

Sample 5 shows one method of organizing the information you discover about a magazine you are interested in.

c. A fortune waiting in foreign markets

One of the cheapest ways to break into print is to write about the area around your hometown and sell those articles to overseas newspapers or magazines. There are English-speaking countries all over the world and English-language newspapers published in countries as far away as Samoa. A quick guide is if the country was ever a British colony, or if it was occupied by British or American soldiers, it probably publishes an English-language newspaper. You, as an overseas journalist, may add a touch of the exotic to their pages. Rick and Barbara once took a visiting Japanese journalist to the Empress Hotel in Victoria, British Columbia, for afternoon tea; the story they wrote about this experience eventually appeared in a national Japanese magazine about English high tea.

Writing articles for overseas publications differs a bit from writing for North American ones. You should use English a bit more formally than you would if writing in North America. Remember, foreign readers may be confused by idioms and slang

SAMPLE 5

Market Analysis

Rover's Daze

A magazine for dog lovers

1. *Rover's Daze*'s advertisements are targeted at dog owners who, although they may have a pedigree animal, are unlikely to be interested in the show ring. Readers of the magazine are generally single or married without children and seeking companionship from their dog. While diamond-studded collars probably aren't in the cards, $75 doggie beds and other luxury items are. Their dogs are taken to the groomer regularly and are up-to-date on their shots. The owners are interested in new ways of maintaining their dogs' health.

2. People read *Rover's Daze* to learn about better ways of caring for their pets. The tone is lively but informative and encourages people to read through it many times. Photos are widely used; every article is accompanied by pictures of dogs with or without their owners.

3. The message the editor is passing along is that dogs, like people, need lots of love and attention if they are going to live long and healthy lives. If you are thinking about buying a dog, *Rover's Daze* will show you how to enjoy and care for your pet.

4. Don't expect to see articles on anything unrelated to dogs, and if you can't write as though you love dogs, forget this publication.

5. Some recent topics include:
   - Canine dental care
   - New methods in obedience training
   - Caring for your aging dog
   - Amazing tale — true life drama
   - Love me, love my dog

   Recurring themes include caring for different dogs, how dogs affect our lives in positive ways, and luxuries for dogs.

6. Most features are written by either staff writers or freelancers whose writing appears in each issue. However, there are at least five short pieces and columns in each issue that are never written by the same person. These are likely an excellent place to break into this market.

that are commonplace at home. If you are already quite familiar with colloquialisms of the country your article will appear in, it will help avoid some hilarious but embarrassing faux pas. In North America, for example, it's quite logical to put your suitcase in the *trunk* when you catch a *lift* to the airport with your neighbor. However, someone from Great Britain could be left shaking his or her head over why those crazy people in the colonies would put their suitcases in another *container* to go up the *elevator*. Of course, to a Briton, it would be perfectly logical to put a suitcase in the *boot* of their car before a *ride* to the airport.

Be on the lookout for likely magazines and newspapers any time you travel abroad or ask your friends to bring a couple home for you. Your local library can also help. Two publications, *Ulrich's International Periodicals Directory* and *International Literary Marketplace*, are chock-full of all kinds of overseas periodicals, general interest magazines, and newspapers interested in articles of all kinds from North America. Reading through all the listings is a daunting task, but it's one that can pay off.

d. Finding market information

Part of any marketing plan includes studying a publication's writers' guidelines and market listings.

1. Writers' guidelines

There are virtually no magazines, regardless of size, that don't provide writers' guidelines to potential contributors. Most newspapers, on the other hand, do not have formal guidelines and you must read the actual newspaper to get an idea of what that paper is looking for.

Writers' guidelines are a detailed summary of exactly what the editor and publisher want and how much the magazine is willing to pay for it. However, the contents and format of writers' guidelines vary, from a conversational three or four paragraphs written in a casual style to several pages of precise information about content, photographic requirements, formatting, editorial preferences, and upcoming topics or themes.

Sample 6 shows some typical guidelines.

Always include a self-addressed, stamped envelope (SASE) when you request writers' guidelines. A standard #10 envelope (approximately four-by-nine inches or 10-by-24 cm) is best. Smaller envelopes mean whoever sends the guidelines back will have to struggle to stuff the paper in; larger envelopes waste postage.

SAMPLE 6

Typical Magazine Writers' Guidelines

The Parenting Challenge
964 Care Street
Babysville, PA 77702
Phone: (464) 555-8484
Fax: (464) 555-5757

The Parenting Challenge is a monthly magazine focusing on issues faced by parents. Our aim is to inform and amuse parents as they go about the business of raising children. Our tone is lively and informative; our readers are inquisitive and expect to learn something new and exciting from each issue.

The Parenting Challenge accepts unsolicited manuscripts, but gives preference to contributors who submit a query first. Please be sure to include a SASE (or SAE with IRCs [international reply coupons]) if you want a reply.

Feature articles: Our preferred length is 1,000 words; however we sometimes accept stories of up to 2,000 words. We need pieces that include information on educational activities suitable for the entire family to enjoy as a group. Special attention is paid to articles demonstrating an "education can be fun" angle.

Inspirational and personal essays are always welcome, provided they aren't preachy.

Tips: New writers may find it easiest to break into the market by submitting personal anecdotes, unusual facts, news discoveries, and short parenting humor to our Parenting Shorties department. Anything newsworthy is considered.

Photographs: Photographs will greatly enhance your chances of getting published with *The Parenting Challenge*. State availability and format of any pictures you have when you first contact us, but do not send originals or negatives unless we request them. Photographs must have captions indicating date, location, and subject, as well as model release forms if necessary.

Payment: We pay $.05 to $.10 per word on publication for feature articles. Payment for fillers and photographs is calculated on an individual basis.

Remember your SASE must have postage issued by the country in which it will be posted.

Guidelines are generally free with a SASE (self-addressed, stamped envelope) and, if you're writing for a sample in any case, why not request guidelines at the same time? This request does not need to be written in lyrical prose. If you set up a standard form on your computer, it is a just a matter of filling in the blanks, stuffing the letter into an envelope, and sending it off with correct postage. Or, you may prefer to photocopy twenty-five or thirty standard letters and fill in the blanks by hand. Either way, Sample 7 shows you just how simple a guideline request letter can be.

All publications change over time, so it's a good idea to date-stamp guidelines as you receive then. Don't worry about requesting new guidelines every year (that's what *Writer's Market* listings are for; see section **2.** below), but if you're basing a submission on guidelines that are five years old, it's definitely worth a phone call to confirm the following:

- The publication is still in business.
- The editor hasn't moved on, retired, or been replaced.
- The publication's requirements (length, themes, style) are still the same.
- The company still hangs its hat at the same address and hasn't moved uptown to the penthouse of a 100-storey office tower.

The most convenient way we've found to store guidelines is in a three-ring binder. It fits easily on the shelf, is easy to update, and the pages don't get lost or misfiled. All you need to do is invest in a set of alpha tabs and you're set.

2. Market listings

There are a host of excellent market listing books available in bookstores or in your library's reference section. These resources put the requirements and preferences of thousands of publications at your fingertips. Some, like *Writer's Market*, published by Writer's Digest Books, are now also available on CD-ROM. See the appendix for more information.

Market listing books provide quick, up-to-date information on a publication's submission format, whether it likes new writers, if your name will be published with your article (a byline), pay rates, reader demographics, and often a few useful insider tips from the editors.

Market listing books are closely related to guidelines. However, there are differences between the two, and we like to incorporate both into market research whenever possible.

Some of the more common differences are —

Letter Requesting Writers' Guidelines

Janet Johns
456 Pen Street
Wordsville, ON M8J 1J9

October 28, 200-

The Parenting Challenge
964 Care Street
Babysville, PA 77702

Dear Madam/Sir:

Would you please send me a copy of your writers' guidelines? I have enclosed a self-addressed, stamped envelope as requested. Thank you.

Sincerely,

Janet Johns

Enclosure

- Market listings usually give the editors' names; guidelines often don't.

- Market listings often state what percentage of a magazine's content is written by freelancers; guidelines seldom include this information.

- Many market listings include a helpful tip from one or more of the publication's editors. These usually take the format of "things we really love to see" or "things we really hate to see." These are worth studying before you submit. Guidelines don't usually offer such tips.

- Market listings may not be current on the editorial slant of a publication, since listings are submitted by publications long before the book is published. Guidelines reflect such changes faster.

- Not all magazines want their names listed in a marketing source book. Some editors feel a writer who has taken the time to write for guidelines will be more likely to submit material appropriate to their needs than someone who has simply thumbed through a book. In some cases, listing in a writers' market book brings such a flood of submissions that the editor (who is more than likely already overworked) prefers to rely on the magazine's reputation to attract writers.

Sample 8 shows a typical market listing.

3. Newsletters, associations, and other information updates

There are a host of association newsletters and magazines aimed specifically at writers. Between us, we have subscriptions to at least a dozen, ranging from a four-page, double-sided newsletter printed at the local photocopier shop, to full-size, national circulation glossies. Although we certainly can't claim to read every word in every one, we do read most of the marketing information in most of the mail that comes through our office door.

The biggest advantage we find with these types of publications is they are just about as current as you can get. There are listings about new markets, publications that have closed their doors, problem markets (usually related to payment), and even contests and grants.

They also usually have some great ideas for improving your writing skills, as well as uplifting articles for those days when you wonder why you ever thought about getting into this crazy profession of writing. Check the appendix for a list of books on the craft of writing.

e. Learn to write a good query letter

At last. You've got your idea, you've done your research and have two or three suitable markets in mind for your article. Now it's time to look for a buyer.

SAMPLE 8
Market Listing

The Parenting Challenge

964 Care Street, Babysville, PA 77702. Phone: (464) 555-8484; Fax: (464) 555-5757. Editor: Big Kahuna. 80 percent freelance written. Monthly magazine focusing on issues faced by parents including education, cultural issues, fitness, and financial challenges. Responds in 10 weeks with SASE. Publishes an average of 6 months after acceptance. Byline given. Willing to work with new writers who show professionalism. Buys first rights. Buys 40 to 50 mss*/year. Length 500 to 2,000 words. Pays $.05 to $.10 a word. Query first.

Nonfiction: General interest articles. We want upbeat pieces slanted toward the North American family with two or more children at home. Keep the tone lively but informative. Articles that concentrate on subjects to increase the quality of life and education for all family members always receive close attention. Humor, inspirational, and personal essays okay.

Fiction: Seldom use. Needs to be something very original for us to even consider it.

Fillers: Anecdotes, facts, newsbreaks, short humor. Buy 100 to 125 mss/year.

Tips: Submit new, fresh information concisely written and accurately researched. Our readers are inquisitive; don't underestimate them.

---

* Manuscripts

"Why should I write a query letter? Isn't it better to just send the whole manuscript so the editor can read it and decide on the spot if he or she wants to buy it?"

"My topic is really hot. If my query letter sits on the editor's desk for weeks, how will I ever get the article out before it's stale news?"

These are just a few of the many questions beginner writers ask themselves about query letters as they begin searching for markets. However, if you want to sell your words to magazines, developing the ability to write a captivating query letter dramatically increases your chances of regular sales.

If you are targeting magazines, here's how to use this invaluable and necessary writing tool.

1. To query or not to query

In any profession, certain conventions inspire intense controversy. In the writing profession, query letters (along with multiple submissions, discussed below in section **3.**) are one of those conventions.

One school of thought says you're wasting your time sending a query letter. Just write the article, submit it, and the publication will either buy it or it won't. Another claims without a query letter, you've reduced your chances of being published by 50 percent or more. While the actual percentages are difficult to pinpoint, here are six good reasons to write a query letter before submitting your article.

(a) A well-written query gives the editor a chance to see a summary of your idea. With a fifteen-minute window of time and the choice of reviewing ten single-page query letters or ten five-page articles, many editors faced with in-baskets measured in feet rather than inches will opt for compact query letters over full-length articles. The queries are simply a more efficient use of the editor's valuable and limited time.

(b) A query letter showcases your writing style and credentials in a single page. If you can capture an editor's attention in 400 words or less, you've demonstrated you know how to write clean, concise prose.

Although you can usually count on a reply to a query letter to a magazine, you will rarely get one from a newspaper. It is better to send the complete article to a newspaper.

(c) Editors like to have input into the format, length, and focus of an article. A query letter, written in advance of the article, gives the editor an opportunity to provide useful direction.

(d) Even if you've done a full market analysis, you can't know what is in the pipeline for upcoming issues. An editor may not be able to use your initial idea, but if he or she is impressed with your writing ability, a query letter may lead to other assignments.

(e) As mercenary as it sounds, there is a financial component to query letters. A single-page query letter weighs less and is, therefore, less expensive to send (and return) than a complete article. The difference between 50¢ postage each way and $1 each way may not seem like much at first glance, but when you're sending out twenty to fifty submissions each month, it adds up fast. Ask any writer.

(f) It is okay to send query letters to a number of publishers at the same time. Again, section **3.** below discusses multiple submissions in more detail.

A note on telequeries: Even if you are uncomfortable doing a telephone query, it may be well worth your time. It can be more expensive (although with the ever increasing competition in long distance rates, this isn't always true), but it's guaranteed to be faster than waiting for the return mail and is more personal than a letter or fax. After pitching two or three well-planned articles, you will start to develop a relationship with the editor. Your name will be more likely to come to mind when he or she is looking for someone to write a piece at short notice. Just remember to make sure you keep the call short and professional and never, ever come across as pushy.

2. Okay, give me five minutes and I'll whip off a couple of query letters

So, you think you can whip off a couple of query letters in five minutes. Think again. Writing a good query letters is an important and time-consuming skill. Unless your idea is exceptionally complex, you have one page, and one page only, to give the editor the abbreviated but still fascinating version of your idea, explain why you are the perfect person to write about the idea you are presenting, and sell the article.

Editors vary on their opinions about telequeries. While some welcome the personal contact even from writers they have never worked with, most prefer not to be contacted by phone until they have developed a relationship with a writer.

Whenever you contact an editor by phone, always ask if it's convenient for him or her to chat for a few minutes. The publishing industry is driven by tight deadlines and, by asking, you show an editor you respect and understand his or her hectic schedule.

(a) Use a catchy opening

Just like the article itself, a good query letter will have a catchy opening that hooks the reader. A useful but often overlooked tip is to use the opening sentence or paragraph of your query letter as the opening to your article. After all, if it has captured the editor's attention, it will most likely capture readers' attention just as effectively. Of all the query letters we send out, more than 75 percent of those that are accepted have used this technique.

(b) Be in the right frame of mind

There's a saying in many writing circles that most writers alternate between thinking they've written the most brilliant passage ever penned and thinking they've written the worst piece of garbage ever inflicted on the literate world. When you're writing your query letter, be sure you're in the former frame of mind.

If you have publishing credits, mention them. Perhaps you've been published in the local newspaper or an organization's newsletter. You may think it's "just a letter to the editor," but it's still a published credit. Perhaps you have special skills or in-depth personal experience in a particular area. For example, who better to write about innovative ways of dealing with hearing disabilities than the mother of deaf twins?

(c) Explain why your article is suitable for that particular publication

Don't make the mistake of submitting an article on divorce to a bridal magazine. If you do, it will be quite obvious you have not given any thought to how the article would fit the magazine's needs. If, on the other hand, you can succinctly explain why and how your idea fits the publication's readership, you will radically improve your chances of being published. Submitting an article on an appropriate topic proves you've done your homework and read the magazine thoroughly before submitting.

(d) Never underestimate the importance of asking for the sale

Many writers present some wonderful ideas, demonstrate they have the necessary background through either study or personal experience, and then fail to ask the editor to consider the article. Although most editors assume they are reading a query, it still leaves a question hanging about why this person bothered to write the letter in the first place. You must explicitly ask for the sale.

Make time to attend press gatherings so you can meet editors of magazines and newspapers face to face. It makes a big difference when an editor can put a name to a face.

(e) This is an interview: look your best

If you were going to a job interview, would you wear ragged jeans and a dirty shirt, and leave your hair uncombed? Probably not. If you want the job, you'll be sure to do everything possible to make a good first impression. You'll dress well, speak clearly, and look the interviewer in the eye as you answer questions. Following standard business etiquette, you will also most likely shake hands when introduced and use the interviewer's name during conversation.

Body language is a powerful way to create a professional, competent image in someone's mind. In fact, studies show approximately 90 percent of communication takes place through body language and tone of voice. Only 7 percent to 10 percent comes about because of the actual words used.

This puts writers at an immediate disadvantage. Writers, after all, have only their words to impress an editor. Since you have none of the communication tools you would have in a face-to-face interview, you must make sure your query letter is brilliant: it is your first and often only way to make a favorable impression on an editor. Before looking at queries in detail, here are a few quick tips to help make your first "meeting" a good one.

There is still some debate about using a serif or a sans serif font for your cover letter. Studies have found most people prefer to read a serif font like Garamond over a sans serif font like Arial. However, another school of thought claims using a sans serif font in your cover or query letter gives it a modern look. Whichever you choose, remember you should always use a serif font for the article itself — no exceptions.

(a) Make sure your query is letter perfect. There should be no typos, spelling errors, or manual corrections. If something isn't right, fix it.

(b) Pay attention to layout and visual effects. Use standard business-letter format and a conventional font such as Times New Roman or Garamond, and forget about fancy colored paper. Lime green paper with a curly-cue font may be fun for family letters, but it won't endear you to busy editors.

(c) Get the editor's name right and use it. If you're in doubt, invest 50¢ and call the publication to confirm spelling and gender. It's hard to maintain a sense of humor when you've just received your 210th letter addressed to Mr. Alex Meyers when you've been a woman all your life. (A friend of Susan's has been struggling with this for years.)

(d) Never fax or e-mail a query letter unless you've been invited to do so. Faxing not only uses up the publication's paper instead of yours (something all businesses object to), but a

See chapter 4 for details on how to format quotations.

fax often takes much longer to get to the appropriate person. And while e-mail is becoming more common, many editors still consider it something of an imposition to receive unsolicited queries this way. Of course, once you become a famous magazine writer with editors lining up outside your door waving lucrative contracts, you can certainly submit in almost any format.

(e) Always enclose a self-addressed, stamped envelope (SASE). Always. If your target market is in another country, remember its post office won't accept a SASE with stamps from your country. An American submitting to a Canadian publication, for example, must supply Canadian stamps.

An expensive alternative is to use IRCs (international reply coupons). IRCs cost up to seven or eight times the regular cost of stamps but are available, and redeemable, at any post office in any country — almost. We recently read about an editor of a trade journal who was unable to exchange IRCs in the small, southern Texas town where she worked. She eventually made the 150-mile (240 km) trip to the nearest major center, where she did find a post office that knew what they were, but now she tosses IRCs in the trash along with the query letter that came with them.

Remember also that Canada and the United States don't use the same measurement for weight. Pull out your calculator and brush up on converting between metric measure and imperial before buying the postage.

3. Multiple submissions

Imagine someone saying to you, "I'm going to give you a brand new car with all the bells and whistles — any type you want — and I'm going to give it to you absolutely free." Would you be excited? Who wouldn't be? So how would you feel if the person making the offer suddenly said, "Oh sorry, didn't I tell you I also offered this to three other people? One of them has already taken me up on it. I've got only one car to give away, so I guess you're out of luck"?

If you are selling one-time rights which allow a publisher to publish your piece only once (see chapter 23 for more details), you could offer your article to several publications at the same time, whether or not their distribution areas overlap. Most magazines, however, wouldn't be interested; they don't want to be just one of three, four, or ten publications you've offered a particular article to. After all, why would they want to publish an article that's appearing simultaneously in their nearest competitor's magazine? A few publications will accept a multiple submission out of hand, but many will not. This leaves you with the choice of either sending a manuscript to only one place at a time, or neglecting to mention you are making a multiple submission.

The first option is honest, but it can keep your manuscript out of circulation for months while you wait to hear back from an overworked editor. The second is equivalent to playing Russian roulette with your reputation. If you are sending out an article to more than one magazine at a time, we recommend you indicate whether or not it is a multiple submission.

Query letters, on the other hand, can be sent out in batches of five, ten, fifty, or more. Why? Because you are offering an idea, not a specific article. Let's say you've decided to pitch an article about a local painter. You query a variety of magazines. One may be interested in a profile of the artist's life, another in the artwork itself, and a third in the investment value of purchasing a painting by an unknown but promising young artist. With the same research and a couple of interviews, you can easily accommodate all three requests with three different articles.

f. Follow through and follow up — politely

Your article is polished, formatted, and in the mail. Now you wait, and wait, and wait.... Sometimes it seems as if your manuscript has fallen into a black hole, never to be seen again. According to the writers' guidelines of the publication you sent your article or query to, the publication responds in two months. But it's been ten weeks and not a word.

A brief, professional phone call is one option. Here are some things to remember before you begin dialing.

(a) Have all the details in front of you: when you sent the manuscript, its title, what subjects were covered, and, most important, the name of the editor you sent it to.

(b) Avoid the temptation to chit chat. This is, after all, a business phone call, not a social one.

(c) If the answer is no, the publication is not interested in publishing your article, accept it without arguing the point. However, if the editor sounds receptive, it's perfectly acceptable to ask what you could have done to make your submission better suited to the publication's needs.

(d) Remember, editors are human. They have off days just like the rest of us. If the person you are speaking with answers your questions in curt monosyllables, it probably has nothing to do with you or your writing ability and everything to do with the pressures of getting a publication out on time.

(e) Another course of action, one many writers find effective, is to send a manuscript status form. These forms make it convenient for the editor to respond and also show that you are a serious writer who is concerned about prompt turn-around. These forms have been known to prompt an acceptance. Sample 9 shows a form used successfully by one writer to track his many submissions to various markets.

g. A note on editing

Newspaper editors need a lot of material every day, and while they need to get the product out quickly, they also have stringent restrictions on space and style requirements. Don't expect to be consulted about changes to your article. In the world of newspapers, most editors simply don't have the time.

Magazine editors enjoy a certain amount of lead time and are slightly more likely to let you know about proposed changes to your article. Some will even send you a copy of the edited article before publication. However, to avoid disappointment and wasted frustration, don't expect to be informed or consulted.

Your chances of having input about changes to your article increase the longer you work with a given publication.

Whichever market you are submitting to, it's important to be aware of and use an editor's preferences for style and slant.

Despite what some people would like you to believe, there are literally thousands of markets for articles of every type and content imaginable. While each market has its own idiosyncrasies, by now you should have a good idea of how to research which markets are best suited to your writing style and interests.

SAMPLE 9

Manuscript Status Form

632 Hopeful Lane
Professionalville, NY 98765

February 20, 200-

Flying Stories
2 Publisher's Lane
Book Town, OR 56789

Dear Mr. Aircraft:

I am writing to inquire about two stories I sent you last November. I'd like to pursue alternative markets for both these pieces if you don't have them under active consideration for publication.

For your convenience, here is a check-off form to help me determine the status of these stories. Thank you for returning it promptly.

On _____, I submitted for your consideration a ms/s called: _____. I have not heard from you regarding its/their status. Would you please (X) the appropriate place(s) in the list below and return this convenient form to me in the enclosed SASE. It will help with tracking/evaluating/marketing my submissions.

( ) If we received your manuscript, we have no record of such.

( ) You included no SASE or one with insufficient postage.

( ) We do not read or return unsolicited mss (SASE or not).

( ) Your story is still under consideration.

( ) Your story is on file for possible future use.

( ) Your story was/will be printed in the _____ issue.

( ) We may have mislaid your ms. Please resubmit.

( ) The following reason:_____

_____

With appreciation,

Mr. Professional Writer

Reproduced courtesy of Arthur G. White.

20

Building Your Career

Twenty years ago, you could still find a newspaper willing to pay for someone's research, time, and expenses, even if he or she was writing only one story for the paper. Now, thousands of amateurs are willing to spend the hours to put together a good story just to see their name in print. Overall, few freelancers are hired to write specific stories on an all-expenses-paid basis. It does happen occasionally, usually for big national publications, and usually for freelancers who contribute regularly to that particular magazine or newspaper.

The spectacular increase in the number of good freelance writers willing to write for fame, glory, and a dime a word means you will have to put in long hours just to have a byline or the chance to learn a new skill or develop a new contact. As a freelancer starting out, the pay you earn will probably just cover expenses — if you receive any money at all.

Syndication has also contributed to the demise of the well-paid freelancer. Newspapers can buy a complete article from a syndication service for as little as $5, so an editor is forced to ask what is so special about a freelancer's $200 article, when that editor could fill the same space for next to nothing.

What this all means is that whether you are contemplating publishing only one or two articles or making a career of writing about your favorite subject, you have to work extremely hard to accomplish your goals. Writing for big bucks right away is almost certainly not in the cards. However, the excitement and challenge of crafting an article is often its own reward.

We have some suggestions for making the most of your time as a word slave. Some of these suggestions are aimed at the writer who wants to make a career of getting published while others are for the occasional writer.

a. Start slowly

1. Start with small community papers

National reputations are always built on local and regional ones. Though they don't pay much, small community papers are always hungry for good writing. There are so many people competing to write for major national magazines the chances of your article being selected are worse than winning the lottery. With persistence you can be published in one of the many small papers and magazines in your region. As your reputation grows so will your credibility. Eventually, as you have enough clips and credits, the national magazines may want your writing.

Occasionally, opportunities do batter your door down and you must be prepared to move quickly and decisively to scoop up an offer. For instance, if a chance comes for you to move to a national or regional stage with a column in a national or regional paper, or a lucky phone call drops an assignment in your lap that will give you terrific exposure, be prepared to re-evaluate your campaign. Don't continue, for example, to try to build a regional reputation if you suddenly have a national showcase that could launch your career as a nationally known writer.

2. Be professional

Even if you have never had an article published, act the part of a professional writer. Dress neatly in business attire and be on your best behavior. If you are invited to an interview or press conference, arrive on time and do a little preliminary research so you have intelligent questions to ask. Unless you're specifically told you can bring a guest, don't. Also, don't gush over internationally famous personalities you meet and be sparing with free wine and liquor. In short, respect your work and your career.

If you are having a hard time getting started on an article, read some of your favorite authors to jump start your brain. One of the wonders of the writing process is what you read doesn't even have to be related to the article you are writing. Good writing tends to beget good writing. Best of all, you can claim to be working when you read your novel.

3. Make it a priority to network

Like every other career, other people in your field can make or break your opportunities. You may not have the guts to call up and invite yourself to events (not a bad talent to cultivate if you can), but there are thousands of things you can do to keep yourself visible. Sending thank-you notes, passing on bits of information, sending notes on new technology or copies of good articles are just a few things even a shy person can accomplish.

4. Get out and about

Go to every event you are invited to even if it is only for a few minutes. While you are there, stay out of tight, little, safe groups of friends and circulate. It is your job.

5. Smile

An upbeat attitude over the phone, at face-to-face meetings, or even in your correspondence marks you as an amiable, co-operative person. Foster this type of image.

6. Perseverance pays off

If you have submitted an article to a magazine you really want to be published in and your article is rejected, wait a bit. Six months from now the editor may need your particular article or a new editor may have the job. New editors like to make their mark as quickly as possible so the fact that the last editor was not enthralled with your musings may actually be to your advantage.

7. You as the expert

As you write and sell your articles, prepare yourself for your television debut. If you are a writer for long enough, you will eventually be asked to give a lecture, do a television interview, appear on an open-line talk show, or be interviewed about one of your subjects for a major paper or magazine.

A lot of cross-pollination goes on in the media. An interesting article lends itself to a captivating radio interview. Terrific pictures (that have accompanied your articles in the past) can do wonders for a limp piece on TV. A question you might field during a radio interview can be expanded in an article.

If you want a career in radio or TV, doing a TV interview will give you an "in": you won't have to do what thousands of hopefuls do and send in an application blind. Your interviews will put you in contact with the right people, and these people will have a chance to see you on air. If you want to lecture about your subject, mentioning a couple of TV appearances on your advertisements for the lecture will fetch a bigger audience.

For all of these reasons, you should spend time each week looking for other media outlets for your writing. It will make you a well-rounded writer, and it certainly will give you more options and alternatives.

b. Set small goals

Set small, realistic goals for yourself. Submit articles to your local paper instead of aiming your queries and articles at the *New York Times* or *Globe and Mail*. These publications receive thousands of submissions each year.

Inquire about submitting articles to small industry newsletters or magazines, local community papers, or local interest magazines. Build yourself a reputation for good work that arrives on time and in the required format.

c. See yourself as a businessperson

Think of yourself as a businessperson whose business is writing. The market for people whose only skill is writing is very competitive and low paying. To stand out from the others, you must understand the business element of what you are doing.

Here's a perfect example from another industry. Who would guess from listening to Loreena McKennitt's harp that she was anything but an ethereal musician? Success obviously came to her because her music is so haunting and inspiring.

Hardly. Just a few years ago she was playing for spare change in subway stations. Although McKennitt's music is a pleasure to listen to, there are at least a thousand equally talented musicians around the world whose music you will never hear. The difference is McKennitt learned a collection of diverse skills to take advantage of opportunities as they arose. She began by retailing her music at concerts and by mail, using money borrowed from friends and family to finance the project. She taught herself how to negotiate her own contracts, sell overseas rights to her music, and set up and implement complex tours.

McKennitt now runs a bustling office. She keeps her sights set firmly on the future, is aware of what's happening in the music industries of other countries, and has plans for using the Internet. On top of all that, she writes and records some truly beautiful music. McKennitt is successful because she likes and works at the business aspect of her career. She admits she spends about 85 percent of her time on business matters.

Even as an occasional author, taking a business-oriented view makes anticipating your editors' wants and needs much easier. As a professional writer, composing good prose may be your most important skill, but to be a success in this industry, it may end up being one of your least-used skills. Writers who view themselves only as writers and refuse to learn about the business are making a huge mistake. With a simple attitude adjustment, you dramatically increase your chances of having your work published.

Further, we guarantee there will be times when you will not be able to earn anything from your writing. Economic recessions, editorial budgets that have been cut, and changing trends within the particular industry you write for will conspire to keep you out of print at some point. If you have diverse skills, you can still be employed doing something else in the publishing or writing field, where you are more likely to hear about or develop other projects.

d. Don't restrict yourself

Always look for opportunities to learn other skills. Don't restrict yourself to the courses aimed at aspiring writers that are put on by many colleges and universities. Try publishing courses or art and photography courses. In fact, any course that makes you organize, write, and express your thoughts better is worthwhile.

And don't overlook a little business education. Most writers wouldn't be caught dead in a tax course, but the knowledge you gain will save you money which you can use for other opportunities. Besides, your understanding of taxes might translate into an article at some point, since everyone pays taxes. If you can show readers how to work with the tax system to save some money, you probably have an article someone will publish.

e. Volunteer

Volunteer anywhere you can where publishing is going on, especially if you are a publishing novice. Real life experience in all facets of publishing is well worth spending time and effort to acquire. These opportunities will give you invaluable insight into the business of writing and publishing — information not available in traditional classroom settings.

There are hundreds of publishers of small newsletters, newspapers, and magazines that barely make enough money to cover their expenses and salaries. They are always looking for assistance in the final stages of preparing the publication for press. Nothing sharpens your ability to find commercially viable projects better than working on several different publications and seeing what works and what doesn't. One easy way to get this experience is to volunteer.

Also, if you are brave, call a respected writer in your area and ask if he or she has a research project you can work on. Make it clear you do not expect to be paid much (if anything). Most well-known writers have several projects on the go at any time. There are never enough hours to do everything and cash is always in short supply. You'll get only one chance, but if you are serious and do a good job for little or no pay, it may get you in the door to more challenging and better-paying projects. Believe it or not, according to several writers we talked to, a good research assistant is hard to find.

Read magazines and newspapers with an analytical eye. This is one place where learning by osmosis really does work. The more you read in your field, the more you'll know what issues editors are interested in and which issues have been done to death.

The long hours you may put in will be rewarded with crucial insight gained at the feet of the master. As someone just starting out, the references, insight, and knowledge your sponsor may give you will cut years off paying your dues.

f. Read voraciously

Read, read, read. There are some very helpful magazines and books available on writing. If you can't afford them, ask your local library to subscribe. *Writer's Market: Where and how to sell what you write* is a valuable source of information published annually by Writer's Digest Books (see the appendix). Most libraries and local bookstores carry copies. *Writer's Market* has an extensive list of contact information on book and magazine publishers. As the directory is updated annually, you can usually depend on it to have current information. However, things change rapidly, so don't expect it to be the final word. We've had letters returned from addresses listed in a current directory.

g. Work in a relevant field

You still need to earn a living while you develop your career as a writer. You may even want to earn your living working in a writing-related industry. For example, working in a printing plant will teach you valuable lessons about some of the basics of publishing. Years later, when you have a terrific book idea or are thinking about starting your own magazine, you will have a good foundation for evaluating whether or not you want to self-publish a manuscript.

h. Start your own publication

We love newsletters as a first publishing effort. Magazines, we don't. The difference between the two is the amount of financial risk you must take to achieve exactly the same thing. Both endeavors will teach you the business of writing and publishing, but a newsletter of say, twelve pages, put out four to six times a year, can be a hundred times cheaper than putting out the same number of issues of a magazine.

Magazines are more expensive for a number of reasons. They generally have more pages than a newsletter, which means added cost for writing, editing, and printing. Distribution can cost more because of the additional pages, especially by mail: the more the publication weighs, the more it costs to ship. However, the biggest difference between a magazine and a newsletter is the production costs. With a newsletter, anyone with a word processor can be in business. If there are any images at all, readers expect they will be black and white, and likely somewhat grainy. Magazines, on the other hand, usually must be in full color to attract advertisers. The color production and printing process is several times the cost per page of a black-and-white newsletter.

When you publish a magazine instead of a newsletter, you will not likely be compensated for the extra financial risk, except you

Being creative about your career path can help immensely in this business. Don't limit yourself to what you think is a traditional route. There is no such thing. Think outrageous thoughts. If you insist on thinking what everyone else is thinking, you will have a harder time coming up with bright fresh ideas that will propel your article to the front pages.

If you have success with a newsletter, expand it slowly. If well presented and marketed, newsletters can become respected vehicles for delivering timely information to the public.

will probably learn how to deal with more stress. For a newsletter, you still need to gather ideas, research and write articles, do layout, figure out how to create a saleable product, and distribute it. These things will be helpful for future projects, regardless of how the newsletter venture turns out. Best of all, you put much less at risk financially with a newsletter.

Try to find a niche. If you can find a niche for your newsletter that is not filled, or even better, a unique marketing plan combined with an old idea, you are on your way. All you need to do to start is publish the first issue. No hunting for start-up capital, no formal business plan (although you should have a good marketing plan in your head), no employees to hire, no government red tape, and no big equipment to purchase.

As a side benefit, you don't need to worry about keeping your writing skills from degenerating while you try to find a publisher for your other work: you have a guaranteed outlet for all you can write.

With guaranteed publication, you will find that, despite your newsletter being small, you will still be invited to press conferences, junkets, and tastings. Everyone knows virtually all publications start small and few companies overlook even seemingly insignificant, new publications because they might later become influential. As a publisher, you will have more opportunities than a freelancer. To get going, and for pointers on production and marketing, see *Producing a First-Class Newsletter*, another title in the Self-Counsel Series.

i.   Buy a byline

We have occasionally heard of writers offering an article to a publication, with the additional offer of paying the publication to print it. And we know of at least once when this has worked well. The article was good, the author needed some publication credits quickly and had money to burn. Violà! Instant bio. (Chapter 22 discusses how to write a bio in more detail.)

There is, however, a wrinkle on this theme: it is fairly common for an advertiser in a magazine to want some editorial content when it pays for an ad. Writers have been known to pay for ads for their business on the condition one of their stories runs in the same issue. For instance, a car parts dealer who has a terrific article about his or her racing hobby might pay for an ad for the car parts store if the article is published in a magazine.

We know this practice will be offensive to writers who think journalistic integrity is paramount, but it is a fact of life in the writing world. Don't dismiss the idea out of hand.

Magazines of all stripes, from one-million-subscriber monthlies to tiny newsletters, survive on the ad-for-editorial exchange. Despite cries of outrage to the contrary, all you need to do is look at many magazines' advertising and then look at who gets a mention in the editorial. (Check the issue before and after the ad too.)

Many writers trying to build a bio volunteer to help a magazine get started, with the implicit understanding one or more of their articles will be published. The magazine gets free help and the writers get bylines. We're not sure we see the distinction between paying with money or paying with noble writing sweat.

j. Just keep plugging

Most would-be writers are stopped in their tracks not by the difficulty of the writing but by not reaching their goal of being published soon enough. Here are some suggestions of how to deal with some of the more common problems. If you pay attention to these difficulties from the beginning and cultivate the right attitudes and habits, you will succeed.

1. Wallpaper with rejection letters

Taped to Susan's computer is a pearl of wisdom she passes on to all her students. She's never been able to discover who the author is, but the advice is priceless.

> Be patient. Be polite. Be persistent. It pays off!
> Forty-eight percent of writers give up after the first
> rejection. About 10 percent resubmit over four
> times. Eighty percent of sales are made after the
> fifth try.

Rejection is part of the business of writing. Never forget it is your successes, not your rejections, that are important. When you get a rejection letter, remember that it didn't appear out of thin air. You had to do something worthwhile to get it — you wrote and submitted an article or an idea to an editor. Maybe the first editor didn't like it, or the second, or the third. But somewhere down the line an editor somewhere *will* like what you're proposing, as long as you're willing to continue sending your words out into the marketplace.

And in the meantime, rejection slips make a unique and inexpensive wallpaper that's guaranteed to be a conversation piece. Display them with pride.

2. "No thanks"

Even the most established writer sends out proposals that are returned with a polite, if impersonal, "Thanks, but no thanks" cover letter. These are the moments when it's vital to remember timing is as important as writing ability. It won't matter how scintillating your prose, a marketplace saturated with stories about gardening bugs isn't going to buy your firsthand experience with the creepy crawlers.

3. Form rejections

It often seems like a slap in the face when an impersonal form letter is the only response after all the blood, sweat, and tears of writing an article. The reality is that editors, especially those who work at large publications, simply don't have the time to write a personalized note. Some don't even bother to send a form letter — we've all received more than one query or submission back with nothing more than a few words scrawled across the top. A few had no indication whether or not the article had even been read — it was just returned.

When this happens to you, and it will, remember that editors are notoriously overworked professionals. It's nothing personal, they just don't have time to write notes to the twenty, thirty, or fifty people who submit ideas and articles to them each day.

4. Learn from rejection

Sometimes an editor may give you an indication of the main reason your idea wasn't suitable for the particular market you targeted. This can be anything from a tick-off-the-box form to a quick note scrawled in the margin of your query. If your idea was very close to the mark, you may even get a short, personal note from the editor. Any feedback you get should be cause to celebrate and learn.

Remember, persistence does pay off. Submitting pieces to the same people over and over again is like a slow, relentless form of torture. Eventually, for relief, they may publish one of your stories.

Always keep yourself in tune with new and unique angles for marketing your articles.

21

Enhancing Your Reputation

Keeping your name in front of editors, fellow writers, and the public, in just about that order of importance, is a job requiring you to promote yourself with some finesse. Few people naturally know how or enjoy selling themselves to the people around them. We are all shy to some degree and none of us are born with the skills to advertise ourselves effectively without appearing to be egomaniacs, but you can learn to do a good job. Once you master these ideas and adapt them to your personality, you will find you get more and better assignments from editors without having to market quite as hard, and fellow writers will think of you when they themselves are unavailable for an offered assignment or trip. You can use these techniques to enhance your standing among colleagues, your boss, and your peers. Essentially, you have to brag a little to get the best payoff for your work but doing it with a bit of class is the most effective way.

a. Promoting yourself with a press release

You absolutely must learn the art of self-promotion to get interviews. There are listeners who will want to hear what you have to say, but unless a talk show host or producer learns about you and your subject, your message, regardless of how important or entertaining, will not reach anyone.

The idea someone will discover you once you have a few articles published is a dream similar to winning the lottery. Before we caught on to how the publicity game worked, we were never invited for interviews. It wasn't the material we wrote. We used the same material for interviews that we had been writing about for years. The difference was the media campaign we launched. To reap the benefits, you must have a plan.

First, come up with several provocative or informative topics. The easiest way to tell if the topics are suitable is to imagine you are the host of the talk show and you are telling listeners what's up next on the show: "And after the news, scuba diver Joseph Calder will tell us about coming face to face with a cave full of skulls on a scuba dive in Honduras." Radio talk show hosts have a well-tuned ear for what listeners want. Would your listeners keep the dial where it is?

Radio announcer: "My next guest has made a small fortune finding rags, well maybe not quite rags, in Salvation Army bins and garage sales and has parlayed them into a multimillion-dollar business. You've heard of the Japanese buying sneakers for $1,000 a pair? Kristin Cross will tell us things to look for in friends' and relatives' closets that are now worth a fortune. Stay tuned after the break."

This role-playing technique works because it takes you out of your usual critical self and lets your subconscious take over. You've heard a million programs. Somewhere in the back of your brain, you know what's interesting. By play-acting as a radio host, you can get a pretty good idea of what will rivet an audience's (or radio host's) attention.

Once you have a theme, grab a piece of paper and boil it down to a phrase or, at most, a sentence. This is the lead for your press release. The shorter the better. As writers and columnists, we are inundated with mail and press releases every day. We do not have time to read it all. If the opening sentence is badly constructed or uninteresting, we throw it out. All the editors and talk show producers we know are under the same avalanche of paper.

Next, in a paragraph, two at the most, give a little more information about your topic. Again keep it brief. Verbiage impedes the message and is a good excuse for the reader to put the press release aside or throw it out. Don't try to tell the whole story here. We usually include background material on a separate page in the form of an article we've written.

Put the lead in large, easy-to-read, bold letters and one short paragraph in normal twelve-point type on one page of your press release. All other background material should be in the package, but on other pages. Sample 10 is an example of a short press release. Note the placement of the telephone number and name.

Don't reuse a dated press release from a month ago to save on printing costs. It is false economy. Editors and announcers throw out anything they feel is so old they will have to check all the information by phone to verify its currency.

b. Developing your contact list

For an initial mailing list, think of all the radio and TV talk shows you listen to and the newspaper columns you read. Once you write a list, call each station and confirm its address and the correct spelling of the host's or writer's name.

We add to our mailing lists all the time. We have a box we throw ideas into, and once a month or so, we sit down and find addresses and enter them in the computer. We also swap lists with other writers who understand this process and create lists too.

Occasionally, we buy a list, but we have never found this satisfactory. Generally, the list is not specialized enough, and we spend days wading through thousands of addresses to pull out the few dozen we might use. Sometimes the lists are too specialized — TV or radio stations in Arizona, for example.

To do the job efficiently, you will need to learn to use a computerized data base. There is no sense in handwriting each address every time you wish to use it. By entering the data into the computer once, you can use it forever.

Almost any computer can handle a data base, so you do not need top-of-the-line equipment. You can also use one of those obsolete nine-pin printers ($30 or less secondhand). The easiest and cheapest labels to use are continuous-feed, single-up labels.

November 16, 200-

Lifestyles or Food Editor:

Press Release

Eat Your Way Around Town for Less!

Who is offering two-for-one coupons in Actionville and the surrounding region? Who is breaking in a new chef or substantially changing their award-winning menu? Our newsletter, *Yummy Eats*, can tell you who. It can also tell you about other promotions that are going on in the world of food. Do you know who has the all-you-can-eat pasta bar on Tuesday nights or where you can eat for less by arriving early?

A subscription is $29 per year.

A sample issue of *Yummy Eats* is enclosed.

Please feel free to reproduce excerpts from any of the enclosed articles.

Contact: Jennifer Michaels

(400) 555-1918

You don't need to purchase expensive laser printer labels, though they do give you a cleaner, more professional-looking printout for a penny a label or less.

Hire a computer expert to set it all up, unless you love fiddling with computers. And don't pay $50 an hour. There are starving students who will do it for you inexpensively. Call the computer department of your local university or the secretarial training school. They will probably know someone who needs part-time work. All those kids who used to type term papers now work with computers and know data bases, so you shouldn't have trouble finding inexpensive help.

If you are not a do-it-yourself type, you could hire a public relations firm to put your name before the public. These firms often do a very good job but they are also expensive. If you've got the money but not the time, hire a public relations firm to organize a mailing list and do your press releases and mailing.

c. Preparing for the interview

Once the media has received your press release, they may want to interview you. This is your chance to put your face and name in front of the public and enhance your reputation.

Print interviews are easy. The reporter asks questions and you answer them. If you don't know, tell the reporter you will find out. The interview may be spread over several days, as you find a relevant background article for the reporter to read, or answer new questions as they come up. Generally, print interviews are more in-depth than those on radio or TV. There is time to do background research and writing articles is a slower-paced process than it is in electronic media.

You'll quickly find print interviews are just another conversation. You still need to organize what you want to say beforehand, but it is less crucial you cover everything the first time.

With radio and TV, you can't stop the interview to look for more information or think about the answer to a question. It may help you to make an outline ahead of time, much as you would when writing an article, but things will always come out of left field in a live interview.

Here's some useful advice to make the most of the interview:

Interviews can be career enhancing. The energy and time you spend on preparing for your fifteen minutes of fame can lead directly to more money and more interesting assignments. When you add the interview to your bio, it also increases your credibility. You are obviously an expert.

(a) Memorize a few points you want to make so the listener will understand the subject easily. Write these up in point form: short, quick reminder phrases. Practice them until you don't leave anything out, but don't make up an entire script of everything you want to say. Unless you are a consummate actor, you'll come off sounding wooden.

(b) Think about the questions you will likely be asked and come up with well-rehearsed answers. You don't think talk show hosts know everything about the people they interview, do you? Sometimes you will need to save an unprepared interviewer from themselves. We have had some really off-the-wall questions because the interviewer thought we were someone else. "So, were the hydroelectric projects in India comparable to ours here?" Uh oh!

We usually try to speak with the host the day before and feed him or her questions to ask. Some see this as a real time saver and are very receptive, while others prefer to wing it on air.

(c) Act naturally, well, as naturally as you can with bright lights in your eyes and someone breaking in to go to commercials every few minutes.

(d) Learn to be long-winded. Simple yes or no answers to questions make the interviewer work too hard to keep the conversation going, and everyone else falls asleep. People love to hear stories, so spice your remarks liberally with anecdotes to illustrate your point. Listeners also like statistics in small doses. Unless you are a professional comedian, never tell jokes.

(e) Watch other shows and see how many times the guests change the tone or the direction of the interview with their answers. Such a skill is useful if the host asks questions you don't know the answer to or that are completely off topic. Just keep returning to the message you want to put across. This requires a little practice, but it is an essential tool.

(f) Try this trick if you need time to think about something: "John, before we get to that, I wanted to tell you about...," and then launch into something you've held in reserve. You can also delay by asking the host to repeat the question if it is particularly complicated. Don't use this with simple questions: "So you wrote this article about living with children with hearing loss?" "Could you repeat that, Dave?"

(g) Let the interviewer know during the break if something is wrong with the equipment. Phone interviews are susceptible to static, and ear pieces do fall out.

(h) Keep any glasses of water well away from you during the interview, especially if you are prone to talking with your hands. If you upset it while making a point, you'll say things not on the FCC and CRTC list of approved broadcast phrases.

(i) Smile. Even if you are being interviewed on radio, it will come through in your voice.

(j) Be careful not to hum, tap your feet, pat the microphone, or talk to yourself out loud. Never, ever, say anything during a commercial break you don't want to go out over the air. The microphone is open more often than you think.

d. Dealing with stage fright

Most of us suffer from stage fright before radio and TV interviews. It is natural to be excited or nervous, but some of us, including actors and politicians, generate enough nervous energy to power a small town. Despite the unpleasant side effects, you will likely still look forward to the experience. It's a thrill.

It does get better the more interviews you do. The first thirty seconds are the worst. After that, most people relax a bit as they become preoccupied with talking and answering questions.

Here are some suggestions for dealing with stage fright:

(a) Take every opportunity you can to put yourself in that threatening place. Every time you succeed, which means simply showing up, not necessarily being brilliant, you become a stronger public speaker.

(b) Join Toastmasters. This organization helps people with public speaking and is a wonderfully safe environment to get your feet wet. Even a few weeks can do wonders for your self-confidence and will give you a lot of practice dealing with your stage fright. If you faint, no one will care. At most meetings, they'll just prop you back in your chair.

Remember, interviewers want you to succeed. We've gone blank on the air, inadvertently given out our home instead of office telephone number, and spoken in an entirely indecipherable language. Each time the interviewer calmly saved us with a long comment or a gentle correction while we pulled it together again. It's their show and their job on the line, so they want to make it sound as professional as possible.

(c) Hum for several minutes before going on air to loosen your vocal chords.

(d) Drink warm water if you need to drink water during the interview. Warm water is better than cold water for relaxing your vocal chords.

(e) Remember to breathe. And do it slowly.

(f) Be aware that your body sometimes betrays you. Your heart beats so rapidly you become nervous because of the physical side effects. Talk to your physician. There are some medications which are great for calming the physical nervous effects without killing your personality. It's important not to let all your energy disappear; you'll come across as lifeless.

(g) Stay away from alcohol or tranquilizers before an interview. You need your wits about you.

e. Getting paid

Unless you appear on a radio or TV show regularly, you are not likely to be compensated for doing so. But once you have appeared a few times as an expert in an area, you should inquire if there is any money to cover your research expenses.

Larger outfits, national broadcasters, or magazines may eventually offer payment if they use you regularly. Smaller companies usually won't, but it is still worth asking. Although regularly paid columns and appearances on TV and radio are coveted and rare positions, they do come up.

Getting one of these positions is a lot like selling an article to a newspaper or magazine. Rather than applying through normal channels, find out which editor or producer is responsible for that particular position. Introduce yourself, and say you are interested in writing a particular column or appearing on air regularly.

Pitch the editor or producer an idea. Your pitch should have all the elements of a press release: a strong idea with a catchy phrase that encapsulates the theme. Send your business card and a bio so he or she knows who you are and what you can do. It helps immensely if you can send something regularly — for example, story ideas you think would be perfect for the show that, of course, you just happen to have written about.

22

Putting Your
Best Face Forward

We used to daydream every editor we submitted a manuscript to was awed by the perfection of our prose, the obvious commercial appeal of our idea, and was scrambling to find a pen to sign a check for us. We would probably have been better off daydreaming about wearing a red cape and blue tights as we hand-delivered the manuscript through the tenth-floor window.

We all want to make a good impression with editors. Even the best, most-established writer needs to pay constant attention to packaging himself or herself in the best possible way. If your manuscript arrives looking like writers' road kill, an editor may pass on tasting the meat of your work in favor of some pristine morsel from the slush pile. Illegible letters and scrawled faxes lacking clear identification send a clear message you don't really care. Editors have too many other would-be authors with neat, concise proposals awaiting their attention to spend time deciphering your messy one.

To give yourself every edge you can, you need to project a competent image and the right impression. Here's how.

a. The telephone

If you are going to use your home telephone line and have other people besides yourself answering the phone, make sure they all answer the phone in a business-like manner and write coherent, accurate messages.

You and the caller must be able to rely on the message-taker to convey the facts to you correctly. If you don't think there is any way in the world the other members of your household can take down a message of more than four words, put in a separate telephone line for your use only.

Answering machines should give the caller a crisp, clean, and short message. Check your machine once a month to be sure the sound quality is still good. Change your tape or message when it needs refreshing.

b. Paper presentation

As a freelance writer, you'll be able to sit at home in your tatty bathrobe and deal with people over the phone, by fax, or by mail. Most days your bad hair day won't sink you, but poorly presented paperwork could. Remember, you are presenting yourself as someone who has a way with words.

Proofread and edit carefully, and use the spell check option on your computer. It should be the last thing you do before printing.

For the sake of efficiency, keep your business letters as short as possible. The shorter they are, the less chance there is to gum up the message. Short, declarative sentences using an active voice and strong verbs are best.

1. Stationery

It is worth your time to put effort into the stationery you choose to put forth to the world. You'll need letterhead, fax cover sheets, envelopes, and business cards. Twenty-pound bond paper is economical and looks good. You don't have to go the route of embossing, color, or heavy-weight stock. Neat and clean is all you really need.

If you have computer software with layout capabilities and a laser printer, there is no reason why you can't create your own business design on good quality paper. Simple designs are best. Look at what other people have done to generate your own ideas. All that is really required is your identifying information (name, address, phone number, plus fax and e-mail numbers if you have them) prominently displayed on the page.

If you are using a typewriter or a basic computer and printer without a selection of print choices (fonts), your options will be more limited. But even with a dot matrix printer, you can still set up basic stationery for yourself. Alternatively, you can go to a print shop and purchase a coordinated stationery package of envelopes, business cards, and letterhead. If you shop carefully and stick with black type on white paper, you should be able to find all you need for under $100.

2. Business cards

Business cards are a necessity. Not only do they give all the information about who you are and what you do in an easily stored format, but more importantly, they convey the message you are serious about what you do.

Try to keep your business card straightforward. Publishing is still a somewhat genteel industry, and fancy titles will not work in your favor. You may be the chief executive officer of your writing company, but everyone will eventually know you are also the mail clerk.

Some creative souls do come up with catchy titles that work. "Rhonda the Writer" is to the point. When in doubt, before you immortalize your title on paper, ask a few business friends if the title you have chosen for yourself is too playful or too grand. Writers with multiple jobs will make it easier for everyone else if they list their various titles.

If you write for a publication on a regular basis, put the newspaper or magazine's name on your business card, not the name of the company publishing the paper. The publisher's name may be relatively obscure while many people will recognize the name of the publication. Be sure you check first with the management about their policy regarding business cards. Regular freelance contributors may have to specify "freelance" to distinguish themselves from staff writers.

Before you have your stationery package printed, ask a friend to proofread it for you. It'll save you reprinting when your e-mail address is missing a letter or you discover some other error you have missed. Talk to your friends in business and you'll find out just how frequently this happens. Unless the error is the fault of the printer, you'll end up paying again. Or worse, an interested editor may be unable to contact you.

You should hand your business cards out frequently, and always have a supply on hand. Include one with everything you mail out, and bring them with you when you visit any trade shows or businesses.

3. Faxes

Fax machines are indispensable for writers and are another opportunity to look good to the outside world. Every fax going out of your office should carry a typed cover sheet with your name, your company's name (if you have one), your telephone and fax numbers, street and e-mail addresses, and some advertising for your business.

Computer fax software comes with fax cover pages for almost every occasion. They are worth checking out — if only for ideas — and many of them can be modified to give your fax a designer look without paying for the services of a commercial illustrator.

c. Your bio

If you want to make a positive impression with an editor, you must let him or her know you can produce great work. The customary way is to send a biography along with your query letter.

Your bio is simply a résumé of your published work — a list of everything you have to your writing credit — along with some other pertinent details about yourself. A bio is usually more specific than a general résumé and doesn't usually include many of your nonwriting jobs. Especially if you are not the world's most gifted self-promoter, your bio will say for you what you would be too embarrassed to mumble in a cold call to an editor: you are professional, finish your work by your deadlines, won't demand too much time, and you know your stuff. Otherwise, why would all these people publish you?

Your bio also gives you credibility as an expert. It should succinctly show your experience. You can use that experience to influence someone to pick up your travel expenses, invite you to a conference, sponsor you, listen to your proposal, read your work, give you an interview, and even lend you equipment.

You will probably have anywhere from two to a dozen different bios with information or layouts tailored for various situations. You might have one that lists all your quotes, interviews, and published articles with details about the theme of the articles and their publication dates. Another might list broadcast experience only. Yet another might simply list the magazine name and the date your article appeared.

Everyone has a different idea of what should be included in a bio. Some purists insist articles or books published are the only legitimate items to include. Others writers also include TV or radio interviews that featured them as the main guest.

In addition to a list of your published works, you may want to list business experience or education relating to your writing. Anything that displays your flexibility, knowledge, and ability to promote yourself is useful in a bio. If you were quoted extensively as an expert, or interviewed for your opinion, or even had a letter to the editor published, you can use this to show your recognized expertise.

The ideal bio establishes you as an expert in your field. A long list of articles published and wide variety of titles show a wide knowledge. Your bio displays the fact that other people value your opinion. After all, they have published, quoted, or excerpted your work.

Don't go to ridiculous lengths when writing your bio. If you've been out of school for more than five years, the editorial columns you wrote for your high school or college newspaper will be more of a detriment than an asset. On the other hand, if you are just out of school, you can consider these as legitimate credits.

The bio shown in Sample 11 is a short overview of the writer's experience, mentioning books written, some selected magazine and newspaper articles, business experience, and education. Note that individual articles are not highlighted in this particular bio.

d. Keeping track

It takes effort, but it's essential to collect and keep copies of all the published articles and tapes of interviews you do. At some point, someone will want to see something you've listed on your bio.

As a matter of routine, you should think about how you are going to acquire copies of any articles or radio, print, or TV interviews that quote you. Don't sit back expecting copies to arrive on your doorstep. It never happens. You need to have a plan to obtain them, and follow through relentlessly.

1. Print media

If an article features your work in a particularly favorable way, you may want to use it as a promotional piece for yourself. We always have copies of two or three favorite articles stuck in the file with our bio so they are handy if someone asks for an example of our work.

MARY JAMESON

Newspaper Columnist

Mary writes a weekly freelance column for the food section of the *Times,* a major daily newspaper in Anytown.

Books Published

Her first book, *Eat Your Way Around the World on the Cheap,* was published in 1996 and is now in its fourth printing. Her second book about cheap and tasty food is scheduled for publication in the spring of 2000.

Magazine Articles

Mary has contributed food and consumer information articles to many magazines and newspapers on a freelance basis.

Television and Radio

Mary has been invited to appear on dozens of radio and television shows across Canada and the United States. Interviews include national broadcasts on ZBC Television's *That's Life Today* and *Foods of the World.*

Teaching

Mary has been teaching food-consuming courses at the college level for the last four years.

Newsletter

Mary edits and publishes a national consumer newsletter, *Recipes for a Dime,* which reports on what to do with leftover pasta and spinach.

Education

Mary has a degree from McGill University in Major Town.

Photocopies of articles are available on request.

1537 Your Street, Anytown   Phone: (600) 555-7654   Fax: (600) 555-7653

Articles in major national magazines or local papers are easy. Go to the store and buy a copy (or twenty, for the relatives). However, obtaining a copy of a newspaper from a faraway destination can be agony. If you have friends there, ask them to pick up a copy as soon as it comes out and mail it to you. Or call a contact in any organization, subject-related or not, you belong to. Alumni associations are often great for this.

Some editors will help, but they are usually so busy they simply don't have the time to make it a high priority. Some papers do send articles out as a matter of course, but more often than not you will need to call the circulation desk and pay for a copy to be sent to you. These costs add up when you factor in the long distance telephone call, the paper, and the postage. It is easy to spend $10 for just one copy of your article.

Magazine articles are usually easier to acquire by directly contacting the editor who worked on your story. The editor is also more likely to automatically send you several copies of the issue you appeared in.

When our first published articles appeared, we each bought more than one copy (but less than a hundred). But we learned after the first few times our relatives had seen us in print, we could safely reduce our cost by purchasing only one or two copies for our files. We quickly found it was expensive to ship a whole magazine. And, as we discovered, most people just wanted a photocopy of the article. We have never been asked by an editor to see the entire publication in which our article appeared.

2. Radio and TV interviews

You will need to plan ahead if you want a copy of yourself in a TV interview. TV stations usually make copies by transferring from broadcast-quality tape to VHS, often with a lot of growling from the librarian who has to find the tape and then from an editor who has to transfer it. TV stations rarely want anything to do with producing copies, regardless of the station's size.

Even if you can't get copies of tapes, keep notes on the date, interviewer, show, station, and contents for your files and bio.

If you are on a local station, your best bet is to tape the show yourself. If it's out of town, impose on friends and relatives to do it for you. Find out exactly when the interview will air. Obtaining a copy of the interview afterward is next to impossible.

Radio stations are generally more agreeable to helping out with requests for copies providing you let them know before the broadcast. After the broadcast, someone has to find the tape of the program and make a copy for you. You are, after all, asking them to do a favor for you, so show as much courtesy as you can and you'll get much better results.

No matter what you do, you won't have copies of all your broadcasts. Get what you can and don't worry about the rest.

3. Organizing your articles and tapes

Some writers prefer to keep their article copies in files with copies ready to send out in a folder behind the original. If you have the space to do this, it can save time, especially if you need to run down to the local photocopy outlet to make copies.

Some writers throw copies in a box in more or less chronological order. When someone wants a particular article, they dig down and make a copy of it.

You may also want to consider cross-referencing your list of published clips in a computerized data base. Just remember the real purpose is to have your copies easily available. Ultimately, whatever method works best for you is the one to use, but be meticulous about immediately adding a notation to your bio. It should always be up-to-date and ready to go. An updated bio also means you have an informal index of all your work.

23

Copyright and Other Legal Gremlins

a. Copyright and your words

Copyright is probably the ugliest ogre most new writers attempt to face down. It is the source of nightmares and chewed fingernails for well over half of new writers and writing students. What happens if someone steals my article? How do I know an editor won't read my story and then assign it to one of the staff writers? What if...?

This book is not meant as a substitute for legal counsel. If you will feel confident your writing is safe and protected only by resorting to costly legal means, then for the sake of your own peace of mind, seek professional advice immediately. And when you reach the enviable stage in your career where publishers and editors are fighting among themselves for the privilege of publishing your work, there is no question you should retain a lawyer.

Until then, while you do need to be aware of copyright law and must be diligent when your rights are infringed, basic copyright is not as terrifying, expensive, or abused as many writers believe. You will save yourself endless frustration, sleepless nights, and money by learning to resist the feeling everyone is out to steal your ideas and your articles.

1. Copyright is automatic

Once you have committed your own, original work into permanent form by writing it down, that work is automatically copyrighted. It is not necessary to indicate copyright with the © symbol in Canada, but in the United States it is. There is probably still some extra protection in showing the copyright symbol, your name, and the year the work was first produced on all your manuscripts even for Canadians. However, some editors we've spoken with (both Canadian and American) feel showing the copyright symbol on your manuscript labels you as an amateur.

2. You cannot copyright an idea

Once you've written it down, the words you have used to express an idea are protected by copyright. No one can use the same words in the same order to describe the same idea without violating your copyright (there are some exceptions to this general rule). However, the ideas themselves cannot be copyrighted. If three people decide to write about building the perfect garden shed or collecting Edwardian silver platters, no one person could sue the other two for copyright infringement unless the actual words used were identical.

3. Registering copyright

For a fee, you can register your copyright.

In the United States, the cost is $20. An application form *and* a copy of the work must be sent to:

The Register of Copyrights
Library of Congress
Washington, DC 20559.

In Canada, the cost is $35 and is submitted to:

Copyright Office
Canadian Intellectual Property Office
Industry Canada
5th Floor, 50 Victoria Street
Place du Portage, Tower I
Hull, QC K1A OC9

An application form must accompany the payment but a copy of the actual work is not required.

While at first glance these fees may not seem expensive, they add up rapidly. If you're producing only one article every two or three weeks, you'll end up spending over $500 annually in either country.

Another option used by some writers is to mail themselves a double registered copy of everything they write. If you elect to use this method, seal your envelope with clear tape and write your signature across the flap. When you receive your manuscript, tuck the unopened envelope away in your filing cabinet or safety deposit box as proof you were the author on the date mailed.

This method is less expensive than registering all your work, but there is some question as to whether it is legally acceptable as proof of original authorship.

4. Work for hire

One exception to copyright principles worth special attention is work for hire.

Let's say Telescope Production and Promotions Inc. (TPP Inc.) wants you to review their newest, most powerful lens for star gazing. In this scenario you will be either:

(a) An employee of TPP Inc. You are paid an hourly or monthly wage from the company, have all the normal payroll deductions taken from your salary at source, and are eligible for any benefits it offers. The sample of TTP's great new product is one of the more exciting perks of employment.

or

(b) You are an independent freelancer hired by TPP Inc. on a per job basis. You invoice TPP Inc., must pay any legally required deductions such as government social security or unemployment plans yourself, and are not eligible for company benefits because you are not an employee of the company.

In the first scenario, your writing is considered to be part of your job, and the copyright remains with your employer unless you have a legal agreement otherwise.

In the second scenario, however, as a freelancer you generally will retain copyright to your material unless you sign away those rights to TPP Inc. If You have any doubts about who retains copyright, ask for clarification.

Since most of you reading this book will fall into the category of independent contractor or freelance writer, this distinction will probably never affect you.

5. Copyright law is constantly changing

Copyright law as it relates to work posted on the Internet is constantly changing.

It's crucial to remember copyright law is constantly changing. Nowhere is this more noticeable than in the world of cyberspace. The legal questions concerning Internet publishing are just being addressed now — a fact causing great concern to all artists. As an artist and a businessperson, it is your responsibility to keep current and aware of copyright law and how it affects you.

b. Selling the right rights

1. First serial rights

By far the most commonly sold rights (especially in the periodical marketplace), the sale of first serial rights simply means you are giving a certain publisher the right to publish your original work for the first time.

With a little thought, it's easy to see you cannot sell first rights more than once in geographical areas that overlap. If you've sold *North America Dog Lover's Magazine* the first North American serial rights for your article on raising bulldog puppies, you cannot sell the first California serial rights to *California Dog Lover's Magazine*. You could, however, sell first Australian serial rights to *Australia Dog Lover's Magazine*.

2. Reprint rights (second serial rights)

Unless your topic is time sensitive, wait six months and then relaunch your already published articles back into the marketplace. Be sure to indicate in your cover letter where and when the story originally appeared and make it clear you are now offering reprint rights.

You can sell reprint rights to as many markets as are willing to accept your work once your story has appeared in print. Many small or regional publications regularly purchase reprint rights. While you will generally make less than you did selling the first serial rights, you don't have to write another article either.

3. One-time rights

One-time rights are generally used if you are selling the same article to several noncompeting markets at the same time. For example, your bulldog article could be published in *California Dog Lover's Magazine*, *New York Dog Lover's Magazine*, and *Yukon Dog Lover's Magazine* within weeks of each other.

The publisher that has bought one-time rights from you can use the piece only once.

4. All rights

Granting all rights to a publisher is a very big step with some very long-term consequences. Once you have signed away all rights, you have forfeited the right to use your article again in any format — including video, movie, anthology, or syndication. You've even given up the ability to use your own words in all future means of production *as yet undiscovered*.

As speculation increases about Internet publishing, some publishers are trying to hedge their bets about what is to come by asking for all rights. We once even ran across an unscrupulous publisher who obtained all rights but offered no remuneration — this is thankfully, a rarity.

Our recommendation about all rights is simple: Never sell all rights unless you are being paid so much money for them you will be able to retire in luxury as soon as you cash the check.

However, that said, everybody has to make decisions without being able to tell the future. Perhaps in two years with the benefit of hindsight giving away the movie rights (included in all rights) to your profile of the latest software mogul won't look so smart. You can try to negotiate your way around it when you sell the article, but if the deal hinges on it, you may decide to give up those possible sources of future revenue in favor of being published now. Your first publishing credits are the most important steps in your career and will open many other doors.

c. The check's in the mail

1. Be sure you know when you will be paid

Most magazines and newspapers pay on publication, that is, a week or two after the article appears in print. From the magazine's perspective, paying on publication means it doesn't have to prepay for editorial copy that may not appear in print for months. From the writer's perspective, it means a wait of sometimes a year or more after submitting an article before there's a financial return for the hours spent writing.

Many writers, quite justifiably, feel this is an unfair practice. After all, they can't market their work elsewhere during this waiting period. Unfortunately, this is common practice and often the only way to get paid anything for your work.

If you can, negotiate to be paid on acceptance and you'll see a check as soon as the publication has accepted your final copy, even if the piece doesn't actually come out until weeks or months later. However, there are very few editors who pay first-timers on acceptance — many pay even regular contributors only on publication.

Occasionally, a magazine will ask for an invoice in order to process your payment. Be sure to check with the editor or accounting department ahead of time.

Regardless of how you are to be paid, your best bet is to stay on top of what is happening to your manuscript. If the paycheck does not appear when it was scheduled to, phone and find out why. Has your article been rescheduled for a later issue or has it been scrapped altogether?

2. The kill fee

No, a kill fee is not the money paid to your survivors if you are flattened by a truck. A kill fee is the amount (usually based on a percentage of the original payment negotiated) the magazine or newspaper will pay you if it decides not to run the article after committing to publishing it. Not all publications pay kill fees.

Sometimes you do not even have to write the article to earn the kill fee. Once, shortly after Rick was assigned an article, the editor left and the new one decided to do something very different with the magazine. Rick received a check without writing a word.

Generally, if an article won't be published, all rights revert to you even if the article was submitted before the publisher decided to kill it. However, be sure to confirm what your contract stipulates — sometimes the kill fee also kills your ability to market the piece elsewhere.

3. When you don't get paid at all

It happens. Your article on investment opportunities abroad is published and months go by without payment. Finally, a crestfallen editor calls to tell you the magazine is out of business and you are now an unsecured creditor of a company with no assets. Or the magazine was purchased by another company and the new and former owners are arguing over who was supposed to pay the writers for previous articles. (Both of the above are true stories.)

You can get mad but you probably do not want to get even. You do have every right to sue and you can sometimes harass owners into paying without going to court. But in this business, it is sometimes smarter to just grit your teeth, smile, and do nothing — tough as it seems.

First, even if you win a judgment, magazines and newspapers usually don't have much in the way of assets. Second, you'll expend more emotional energy trying to recover your paycheck than it is worth. You could spend the same energy much more positively advancing your career by finding another buyer for your article. And third, editors do not go down with the company. They move to other magazines where they will hire you because they know that not only do you write publishable work, you are a kind and understanding sort who gave them a break in one of their more embarrassing moments.

d. Read the fine print — what's negotiable

Because magazines often contract for articles months ahead of publication, there is usually a bit more time to negotiate the terms of the sale than when you're dealing with a newspaper. Don't be afraid to ask for changes to your contract.

Many magazines don't use written contracts and rely on a verbal agreement between writer and editor. While reputable publications will follow through, be aware that verbal contracts are harder to enforce in the case of a disagreement. There can also be problems with how each person interprets what was said in the verbal agreement.

To protect yourself from confusion, write a letter outlining the terms as you understand them and mail it off to the editor. Make sure you spell out the deadline, payment, subject, and length of the article and the rights you are selling. At the end of the letter, write, "If this is not what we have agreed, please let me know right away." Keep a copy for your files. Sample 12 is an example of a letter outlining the terms of an assignment agreement.

One of the sad truths about writing is many authors do not see themselves as businesspeople. Somehow the idea they must learn about the legal aspects of what they do seems to diminish the lustre of their career. However, writers who accept this as just one of the many skills they need are generally the ones whose careers shine brightest.

SAMPLE 12

Letter of Assignment Confirmation

Lois Writer
900 Druid Street
Eatonville, ON Z4V 2B4

August 15, 200-

Mr. R. Matthew
Managing Editor
Yummy Eats
375 Mayne Street
San Francisco, CA 99887

Dear Mr. Matthew:

I am so pleased you like the hook in the first line of the story. I am really excited about the prospect of writing a 1,000-word article entitled "Where to Find the Best Barbeque in Texas" for your "Eating Around" column for the May 1, 200- issue of *Yummy Eats*. The article will give readers specific restaurant recommendations and the sidebar will contain at least one hot and hearty recipe.

I understand that the deadline for submission is November 1, 200-. The payment is $500 and I am to bear all research costs. You are purchasing first serial rights for North America only and there is no kill fee.

If this is not what we have agreed, please let me know right away.

Cheers,

Lois Writer

Appendix

a. Useful resource publications

Books in Print
An up-to-date version of this comprehensive reference book of titles in print is available at most libraries.

Canadian Markets for Writers and Photographers
Proof Positive Productions
#1330 – 194 – 3803 Calgary Trail
Edmonton, AB T6J 5M8
Difficult to find and hasn't been recently updated, but comprehensive and easy to read.

Canadian Writer's Market
McClelland and Stewart
481 University Avenue
Toronto, ON M5G 2E9
Lists magazines, book publishers, literary agents.

Gale Directory of Publications and Broadcast Media
Gale Research
835 Penobscot Building
Detroit, MI 48226-4094
Toll free: 1-800-877-4253
Tel: (313) 961-2242
Fax: (313) 961-6083
Extensive but expensive. An up-to-date version of this reference book is available at most libraries.

Quill and Quire
70 The Esplanade, 2nd Floor
Toronto, ON M5E 1R2
Tel: (416) 360-0044
Fax: (416) 360-8745
Monthly journal for the Canadian book trade.

The following six publications are available from R.R. Bowker
(see address below) or from the reference section of the library:

- *Books in Print Database*
- *International Literary Market Place*
- *Literary Market Place*
- *Publishers, Distributors and Wholesalers of the U.S.*
- *Publishers Trade List Annual*
- *Ulrich's International Periodicals Directory*

R.R. Bowker
121 Chanlon Road
New Providence, NJ 07974
Toll free: 1-800-521-8110
Tel: (908) 464-6800
Fax: (908) 665-6688

Standard Periodical Directory
Oxbridge Communications
150 Fifth Avenue, Suite 302
New York, NY 10011-4311
Tel: (212) 741-0231
Fax: (212) 633-2938

The following three books are updated annually and are available
from *Writer's Digest Books* (see address below):

- *Writer's Market: Where and how to sell what you write*
- *Photographer's Market*
- *Guide to Literary Agents*

Writer's Digest Books
F and W Publications
1507 Dana Avenue
Cincinnati, OH 45207
Toll free: 1-800-543-4644
Tel: (513) 531-2222
Fax: (513) 531-4744

Writer's Digest Magazine (monthly)
P.O. Box 2124
Harlan, IA 51593-2313
Tel: 1-800-333-0133 (Subscription department)
Fax: (515) 246-1020

b. Organizations for Writers

American Society of Journalists and Authors
1501 Broadway, Suite 302
New York, NY 10036
Tel: (212) 997-0947
Fax: (212) 768-7414

Authors League of America
330 West 42nd Street, 29th Floor
New York, NY 10036
Tel: (212) 564-8350
Fax: (212) 564-8363

Canadian Association of Journalists
St. Patrick's Building, Room 316B
Carlton University
Ottawa, ON K1S 5B6
Tel: (613) 526-8061
Fax: (613) 521-3904

Canadian Authors Association
320 South Shores Road
P.O. Box 419
Campbellford, ON K0L 1L0
Tel: (705) 653-0323
Fax: (705) 653-0593

International Food, Wine and Travel Writers Association
P.O. Box 13111
Long Beach, CA 90803
Tel: (310) 433-5969
Fax: (310) 438-6384

International Women's Writing Guild
P.O. Box 810, Gracie Station
New York, NY 10028-0082
Tel: (212) 737-7536
Fax: (212) 737-9469

National Writer's Association
3140 S. Peoria St. #295
Aurora, CO 80014
Tel: (303) 841-0246
Fax: (303) 751-8593

National Writers Union
113 University Place, 6th Floor
New York, NY 10003
Tel: (212) 254-0279
Fax: (212) 254-0673

Periodical Writers Association of Canada
54 Wolseley Street, 2nd Floor
Toronto, ON M5T 1A5
Tel: (416) 504-1645
Fax: (416) 703-0059

Society of American Travel Writers
4101 Lake Boone Trail, Suite 201
Raleigh, NC 27607
Tel: (919) 787-5181
Fax: (919) 787-4916

Writers Guild of Canada
Third Floor North — 35 McCaul Street
Toronto, ON M5T 1V7
Toll free: 1-800-567-9974
Tel: (416) 979-7907
Fax: (416) 979-9273

Writers' Union of Canada
National Office
24 Ryerson Avenue
Toronto, ON M5T 2P3
Tel: (416) 703-8982
Fax: (416) 703-0826

c. Books on the craft of writing

Elbow, Peter. *Writing without Teachers.* 2nd ed. Oxford: Oxford University Press, 1998.

Elbow, Peter. *Writing with Power.* 2nd ed. Oxford: Oxford University Press, 1998.

Fryxell, David. *How to Write Fast While Writing Well.* Cincinnati: Writer's Digest Books, 1992.

Miller, Casey, and Kate Swift. *The Handbook of Non-Sexist Writing.* New York: Lippincott & Crowell, 1980.
This book is currently out of print, but worth watching for in secondhand bookstores.

Ross-Larson, Bruce. *Edit Yourself: A Manual for Everyone Who Works With Words.* New York: W.W. Norton, 1996.

Strunk, William, and E. B. White. *The Elements of Style.* 3rd ed. New York: Macmillan, 1979.

Zinsser, William. *On Writing Well: The Classic Guide to Writing Nonfiction.* 6th ed. New York: Harper Reference, 1998.

Writing Travel Books and Articles

by Richard Cropp, Barbara Braidwood, and Susan M. Boyce

$15.95

If you love to travel and have a way with words, travel writing could be your perfect opportunity! Offering guaranteed job satisfaction and cheap or free travel, travel writing has many fringe benefits — getting behind-the-scenes information, achieving recognition as an expert, and traveling to your favorite destinations as often as you wish are just a few. This complete guide is ideal for the novice writer, but is also full of helpful tips for the experienced travel writer.

- Written by travel-industry experts
- Reap the benefits of becoming a travel writer
- Discover the different types of travel writing
- Create a distinctive style
- Get your article published
- Contains plenty of samples

Order Form

All prices are subject to change without notice. Books are available in book, department, and stationery stores. If you cannot buy the book through a store, please use this order form.

(Please print)

Name_____

Address_____

Charge to: ❏ Visa ❏ MasterCard

Account number _____

Validation date _____

Expiry date _____

Signature _____

YES, please send me:

____ *Writing Books for Kids and Teens*

____ *Writing Cookbooks*

____ *Writing Travel Books and Articles*

❏ Check here for a free catalogue

Please send your order to the nearest location:

IN THE U.S.A.
Self-Counsel Press Inc.
1704 N. State Street
Bellingham, WA 98225

IN CANADA
Self-Counsel Press
1481 Charlotte Road
North Vancouver, BC V7J 1H1

Self-Counsel Press
4 Bram Court
Brampton, Ontario L6W 3R6

Visit our Web site at:
www.self-counsel.com

OTHER TITLES IN THE SELF-COUNSEL WRITING SERIES

Writing Books for Kids and Teens
by Marion Crook
USA $12.95   CDA $15.95

Marion Crook, the author of nine novels for children and teens, provides a systematic approach for new and published writers alike. Using extensive examples, Crook considers the elements and craft of writing for this readership. Contents of the book include the basic ingredients of a story, ethics and morality, writing for different age groups, and marketing the story.

- Considers both fiction and nonfiction

- From picture books to young adult

- Explores the differences in writing for various age groups

- Provides extensive examples to illustrate elements of writing

- Includes worksheets to help writers plan their work

Writing Cookbooks
by Judith Comfort
$15.95

Do you have a favorite series of recipes and a flair for cooking? Why not create and publish your very own cookbook? Be it a collection of grandmother's recipes, a culinary history of an ethnic background, or a thousand-and-one ways to eat a favorite staple, there is a huge and varied market for new cookbooks. This complete guide includes:

- Developing and researching your cookbook concept

- Collecting and testing recipes

- Writing recipe introductions

- Preparing a book proposal

- Marketing tips for fundraising cookbooks